# The Complete Multifaith Resource for Primary Religious Education

*The Complete Multifaith Resource for Primary Religious Education Ages 4–7* is a definitive teaching and learning aid for cross-religious exploration in the classroom, offering stimulating and detailed ways in which to apply a concepts-based approach to the teaching of RE. It provides a model for learning which engages children and encourages the development of higher-order thinking skills, which can be applied to other subject areas in cross-curricular settings.

Comprising a book and CD-ROM, *The Complete Multifaith Resource* features key concepts that underpin religious beliefs and practices and that are key to effective learning in RE for the target age level. Each concept chapter provides a wealth of material which will enable teachers to lead their pupils through the learning experience. Resources can be displayed on an interactive whiteboard for classroom viewing, or alternatively printed out for pupils to use during individual and group activities, requiring no further search for material. This includes:

- stories, pictures and questions to prompt discussion
- writing frames, sort cards, matching pairs and other engaging activities

This indispensable tool provides a modern, innovative and refreshing approach to teaching RE that has already proved to be effective in a large number of schools, and can be applied to the effective delivery of an agreed syllabus for RE. Each chapter is introduced by looking at the key concept from a Christian point of view, and is then examined from the perspectives of the other major world faiths, including Buddhism, Judaism, Islam, Hinduism and Sikhism.

*The Complete Multifaith Resource for Primary Religious Education Ages 4–7* will be of value not only to RE managers and leaders, but also to primary phase teachers who may have little confidence or expertise in teaching RE. Trainee teachers and those studying on education courses will also benefit from gaining a better understanding of the concepts-based approach to the teaching of RE as expounded by the Hampshire, Portsmouth and Southampton Agreed Syllabus.

**Judith Lowndes** is currently a general inspector for primary RE in Hampshire. She has extensive experience of teaching primary pupils and advising on religious education provision, and has lectured on religious education provision to students and trainee teachers in higher education. She has contributed to a number of RE book of *Primary Religious Education – A New Approach*, also published by

# Acknowledgements

Acknowledgements are due to Hampshire County Council, Hampshire SACRE and Hampshire, Portsmouth and Southampton teachers who have worked with some of the material included in this book. Any works included that were previously published by Hampshire County Council are under its copyright and are included with its permission, by licensed agreement.

Particular acknowledgements are due to Clive Erricker who is a friend and, until recently was my colleague. The conceptual enquiry approach and methodology that this book recommends is his brainchild. We worked on implementing the methodology in schools over a number of years, and the material in this book is my attempt to support teachers in applying this particular approach effectively in their classrooms.

# The Complete Multifaith Resource for Primary Religious Education
## Ages 4–7

Judith Lowndes

Routledge
Taylor & Francis Group

LONDON AND NEW YORK

First published 2012
by Routledge
2 Park Square, Milton Park, Abingdon, Oxon OX14 4RN

Simultaneously published in the USA and Canada
by Routledge
711 Third Avenue, New York, NY 10017

*Routledge is an imprint of the Taylor & Francis Group, an informa business*

*British Library Cataloguing in Publication Data*
A catalogue record for this book is available from the British Library

*Library of Congress Cataloging in Publication Data*
Lowndes, Judith.
 The complete multifaith resource for primary RE : ages 4-7 / Judith Lowndes.
 p. cm.
1. Religious education of children. 2. Education, Primary. 3. Christianity and other religions--Study and teaching. I. Title.
 BV1475.3.L69 2011
 200.71--dc22
  2011011711

ISBN: 978-0-415-66867-5 (pbk)
ISBN: 978-0-203-81637-0 (ebk)

Typeset in Helvetica
by Saxon Graphics Ltd, Derby

Illustrations by Gary Holmes

MIX
Paper from
responsible sources
FSC
www.fsc.org    FSC® C004839

Printed and bound in Great Britain by the MPG Books Group

# Contents

# Introduction

This publication provides an approach for teaching religious education (RE) which has proved to be effective in a large number of schools. It focuses on an enquiry into concepts or key ideas, and employs a particular cycle of learning that can be applied to locally agreed syllabuses for religious education. This book and accompanying CD look at RE specifically, but in the units of work teachers will see opportunities to apply the methodology to and make links with other curriculum areas. This is particularly valuable for those schools seeking to develop cross-curricular skills to improve pupils' learning. Teachers in the Foundation Stage will recognise the potential for making links with Early Years and Foundation Stage (EYFS) requirements, enabling them to structure children's learning alongside material that emanates from their particular interests.

This approach was originally developed to inform the production of the agreed syllabus for RE in Hampshire, Portsmouth and Southampton, and was later adopted by Westminster's local authority. As a result it has been tried and tested by hundreds of teachers in the south of the UK with great success. Recent research carried out in Hampshire, Portsmouth and Southampton schools (The Living Difference Evaluation Project Report by Katherine Wedell, February 2009, published by Hampshire County Council) indicates that pupils and teachers are enthusiastic about this approach to RE. Evidence shows that pupils' attainment in RE is improved as a result.

## Why focus on concepts?

Religious education has a legacy of developing learning through exploring religious material such as important figures, festivals and celebrations, stories, beliefs and practices. The focus has often been on acquisition of knowledge. For example, a class of young pupils may be exploring the Jewish festival of Passover. They hear the story of Moses leading the Israelites out of Egypt and act it out in the hall, they create art work for a display in the classroom illustrating the ten plagues, they explore and make Seder plates, and they role play a Jewish family celebrating the Passover meal. Teacher and pupils have had a great time. The emphasis, however, has been on what Jews do at Passover, often with less attention on why Jews participate in the rituals and celebrations. Although pupils have been fully engaged with the lessons, the information about Passover may have no point of resonance with young pupils, and as a result, there may be limited understanding of why Jewish people would engage with such activities.

The approach in this book recommends that teachers should focus on one of several potential concepts (key ideas) that underpin the religious material that has been selected. As children engage, in detail, with the particular concepts, they are in a position to relate to the concept themselves, make sense of the concepts within their own experience, and be in a better position to recognise the significance of that concept for the particular religious people being explored. This particular approach enables young pupils to recognise and gain insight into the meaning and significance of human behaviour, both religious and non-religious.

In relation to the example of the festival of Passover, the concept of *remembering* is one that younger children can grasp and recognise within their own lives, and one of several that are of significance for Jews at Passover. Using the cycle of learning that this book demonstrates, therefore, would enable young pupils to reflect on what they themselves like to remember and how they remember things. They would consider how *remembering* can affect their lives and how remembering affects others too, in different and similar ways. They would explore how people *remember* things, through listening to stories, seeing pictures, singing songs or eating special foods, for example. At this point young pupils would explore what and how Jews *remember* at the festival of Passover. Young pupils engage with the story, the songs, and the special food that help Jews to remember how God has looked after them in times of need. Young pupils would be encouraged to consider and reflect on the importance of remembering for Jews in relation to their own experience.

## Which concepts should we focus on?

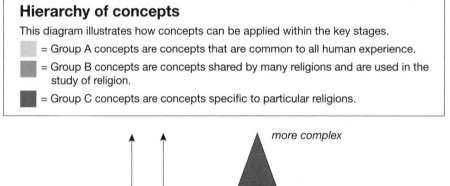

**Hierarchy of concepts**

This diagram illustrates how concepts can be applied within the key stages.

■ = Group A concepts are concepts that are common to all human experience.

■ = Group B concepts are concepts shared by many religions and are used in the study of religion.

■ = Group C concepts are concepts specific to particular religions.

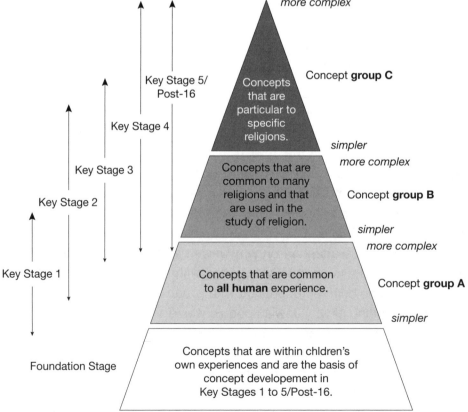

*Figure 0.1*

Within the Foundation Stage and Key Stage (KS) 1, teachers appreciate the importance of engaging the children in familiar territory and then extending their experience and understanding. With that in mind, this publication illustrates how children can enquire into simple concepts or key ideas that are part of common human experience. These are classified as group A concepts (see the cycle of learning diagram on page 2 Figure 0.1). In this category are the concepts of *remembering*, *belonging*, *storytelling*, *authority*, *special* and *celebration*. There are many more concepts in this category. Many are simple and suitable for very young children, while some are more sophisticated, such as *freedom*, *justice* and *prejudice*. These would be better approached with older pupils in KS2 or KS3.

Group B concepts are those that are common to many religions (see Figure 0.1) such as *holy*, *worship*, *disciple* and *God*. These concepts are more challenging as they engage pupils in figurative language, and they are more frequently introduced at KS2. Group C concepts are those that are exclusive to each of the religious traditions, such as *dukkha*, *resurrection*, *umma*, *sewa*, *darshan* and *mitzvot*. These very specific religious concepts require a more sophisticated level of engagement and interpretation. Some of these concepts can be effectively introduced at the top of KS2 and on into KS3 and KS4. Examples of teaching and learning approaches to group B concepts are provided in the companion book for the 7–11 age range.

## What is the cycle of learning for?

The cycle of learning is a particular methodology which provides a structure that enables children to focus on and enquire into a concept. Teachers will recognise some of the strategies and techniques employed within the cycle that can make a strong contribution to developing thinking skills. The methodology engages children in thinking beyond basic recall, and encourages children to engage with and develop higher-order skills such as reflection, speculation, categorisation, application, evaluation and analysis. The methodology enables pupils to grow in their understanding of concepts and recognise their significance within their own experience and the experience of religious people. This approach to RE is to enable children to *interpret religion in relation to human experience*. Those teachers who work with an agreed syllabus that requires pupils to *learn about religion* and *learn from religion* find that this methodology provides a meaningful focus and link between the two attainment targets.

## How does the cycle of learning work?

The cycle of learning diagram illustrates how the methodology works and the purpose of each element of the cycle of learning. Readers will find this diagram at the start of each unit of work, demonstrating some key questions for each element in relation to the identified concept.

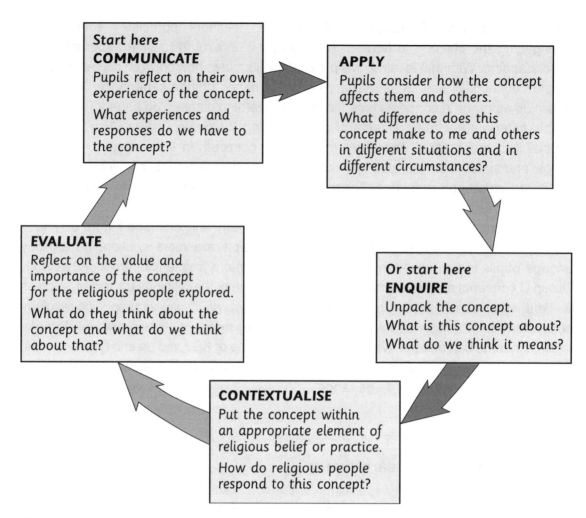

*Figure 0.2*

### Communicate

When the concept or key idea is simple and children are in a position to talk about, share and reflect on their own experience of a concept, this is a useful place to start. Teachers of younger children will often want to provide a stimulus with which children can identify, and this will engage their thinking and promote discussions. There will often be a reinforcement activity here such as circle time, art and craft work, drawing and annotating, or perhaps role play.

### Apply

This section is closely linked to and develops out of **communicate**. In this section the teacher should challenge the children to think beyond their initial responses. How does the concept affect them in their lives? Does everyone think the same way about this concept? Does everyone have the same experience? Will they always feel like this about the concept? Do they think that they might feel the same in different circumstances? Paired talking and group discussion work well here, and so does role play, or teachers may want to provide a simple drawing or writing frame for children to complete.

### *Enquire*

In this section the teacher leads the children to explore a broader interpretation of the concept. For example, pupils will have been able to share their own experiences of belonging (within **communicate**), but here the teacher could provide pictures or cards to help children to identify things that help people to feel that they belong. For some concepts this may be the ideal starting point. If the concept is less familiar to children, teachers should illustrate the concept to help children unpack its meaning. The concept of *authority* is more challenging, and in this book the starting point is **enquire**. Brainstorming (with an adult scribe if required) or concept mapping, sorting and categorising words, listing features, and group or class speaking and listening are useful techniques for this section.

### *Contextualise*

Here the teacher draws on religious material to illustrate how people of that faith respond to the concept. The simple concepts used within the Foundation Stage and KS1 (from the group A category in Figure 0.1) provide enormous potential. For example, if the concept is *celebration*, the possibilities are endless. In this book a suitable aspect of the religion has been selected, which provides a tangible and accessible example of a religious response to the concept. In this **contextualise** section children can be involved in visits, speaking to visitors, art and craft work, cooking, music, dance, drama and so on. The use of persona dolls, explained later in this introduction, is particularly useful in this element of learning. It is particularly important within this part of the cycle to keep the concept at the centre of learning. It is not acquisition of knowledge that is important here, but fundamentally about children recognising the importance of the concept to religious people.

### *Evaluate*

This section emanates from and is very closely linked to **contextualise**. Here children are encouraged to reflect on why the concept is important to those people that have just been investigated, and what difference it makes to their lives. Visitors are particularly valuable, and also the use of persona dolls. A useful approach to generate some thoughtful responses from children is to ask them to imagine that the persona doll (or visitor) does not have something (a special book, a celebration, a place where they belong, etc.) and how that makes them feel. Children should also be encouraged to articulate their own opinions in this section. What do the children in the class think about the concept and its value? Do they agree or disagree with the persona doll or the visitor? Discussion, role play, hot seating and completing speech bubbles, simple debates and voting are helpful strategies to employ within this section.

## How to use this publication effectively

In this book you will find the concept-led enquiry approach applied to six different concepts. They are all contextualised within aspects of Christianity, which all teachers should find useful as it is a legal requirement that Christianity is taught in all key stages. Each concept is also contextualised within aspects of other major world religions (Buddhism, Hinduism, Judaism, Islam and Sikhism) where appropriate. The accompanying CD provides support material, pictures, drawing and writing frames, which can be used on the whiteboard or duplicated and used as hard copies to support the teaching and learning. Teachers may:

- Follow the guidance in the book for a particular concept in relation to Christianity, going through all the elements in the cycle (**communicate**, **apply**, **enquire**, **contextualise** and **evaluate**). They can then go to the material provided for the other religion on which they wish to focus to illustrate the same concept within the **contextualise** and **evaluate** elements of the cycle.
- Follow the guidance for the **communicate**, **apply** and **enquire** elements in the book for a particular concept, then go to the material about the religion on which they wish to focus to follow the **contextualise** and **evaluate** elements, for that concept, leaving out the Christian dimension on this occasion.

It is not appropriate to exemplify every concept within all religions, because the concept may not be of the same significance in every religion. Illustrative material has been included where there are appropriate and accessible examples from the religions identified.

Teachers will need to consult their locally agreed syllabus for RE in order to find out which religion they should be exploring in the Foundation Stage and KS1. If the agreed syllabus requires that a school chooses a religion to explore, it is recommended that children should consistently meet aspects and examples of that religion within Foundation Stage and KS1 so as to help them develop a coherent picture of that religion alongside their learning about Christianity. Experience tells us that dropping into a number of different religions can cause confusion.

The units have been planned so that children progress in their understanding as they move through the cycle of learning. The correct order and inclusion of all the five elements in the cycle is essential for effective learning. There are two potential starting places: **communicate** or **enquire**. The appropriate starting points have been identified as 'Step 1' in each cycle of learning in this book.

## Using persona dolls

'Persona doll' is the name given to a child-sized rag doll produced by a company that trades under that name. The term 'persona doll' also appears to be a generic term used for various sorts of dolls utilised in the classroom to support learning. The doll is used to enable young children to engage with issues that are or may be of concern to them, but they do so vicariously through the doll. Therefore, the doll may have been bullied in the playground, or may have a new baby brother, or may have a granddad who has just gone into hospital. More recently teachers have recognised the contribution the dolls can make in religious education.

Teachers may find that they have a limited range of different beliefs or cultures represented in their classes, or they may find that pupils from minority groups are reluctant to share the beliefs and practices of their families in school. The use of a persona doll enables the teacher to engage the children with a particular faith through the imaginary experiences of the doll who is a member of that faith. Teachers give the doll a name, a home near the school, a family, pets, favourite foods and interests. The persona doll becomes a member of the school and is the same age as the pupils. When the children engage with a particular concept, within the **contextualise** and **evaluate** elements of the cycle of learning, they can do so through the experiences of the persona doll. Children therefore learn about the persona doll's special book, or place where he or she feels that he or she belongs, or the way that a festival is celebrated, and so on. The doll does not speak (no ventriloquist skills are required), but whispers to the teacher, who explains to the class what the doll wishes to share.

It is recommended that infant schools should have a Christian persona doll and one to represent another of the faith(s) that are in focus in the Foundation Stage and Key Stage 1. Further guidance and details about purchasing and using persona dolls can be found on the following websites:

www.persona-doll-training.org
www.articlesoffaith.co.uk/
www.parrotfish.co.uk

Also see *The Little Book of Persona Dolls* by Marilyn Bowles (Featherstone Education, 2003).

## Units of work in this book

| | |
|---|---|
| Belonging | Foundation Stage and Key Stage 1 |
| Celebration | Foundation Stage and Key Stage 1 |
| Remembering | Foundation Stage and Key Stage 1 |
| Special | Key Stage 1 |
| Authority | Key Stage 1 |
| Storytelling | Key Stage 1 |

## Religious characters

A. Joe, a Christian boy

B. Elsa, a Buddhist girl

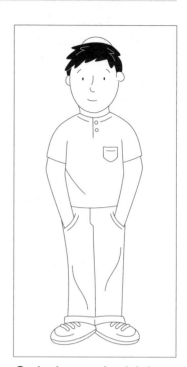

C. Joshua, a Jewish boy

D. Sita, a Hindu girl

E. Fatima, a Muslim girl

F. Amjid, a Sikh boy

# Belonging

The concept of *belonging* is one that is fundamentally important in young children's lives, and naturally emanates from their own interests and enquiries. Exploring this concept or key idea in religious contexts will broaden children's experiences and enable them to make wider connections, forming the foundation for enquiring into the concept *community* or *identity* in Key Stage 2. This unit explores the concept *belonging* in the context of what helps Christians feel as though they belong in a church, and focuses on the ideas of shared values, mutual support, familiarity with surroundings and activities, and where Christians frequently find that they feel comfortable. It also provides examples of how *belonging* can be explored within aspects of other major religions.

What helps Buddhists feel they *belong* in a temple?
What helps Hindus feel they *belong* in a mandir?
What helps Jews feel they *belong* in a synagogue?
What helps Muslims feel they *belong* in a mosque?
What helps Sikhs feel they *belong* in a gurdwara?

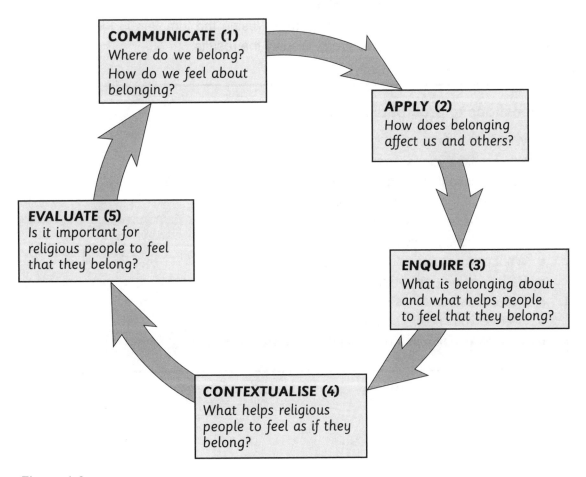

**COMMUNICATE (1)**
Where do we belong?
How do we feel about belonging?

**APPLY (2)**
How does belonging affect us and others?

**ENQUIRE (3)**
What is belonging about and what helps people to feel that they belong?

**CONTEXTUALISE (4)**
What helps religious people to feel as if they belong?

**EVALUATE (5)**
Is it important for religious people to feel that they belong?

*Figure 1.0*

## Belonging in Christianity

### *Step 1 Communicate*

### Where do we belong? How do we feel about belonging?

- Teacher shows the children a picture of his/her house and explains that this is where s/he feels that s/he *belongs.* Teacher asks children to think about how s/he knows that s/he *belongs* there (for instance: my things are there, my books, my bed, my chair, my television). Teacher asks the children where they *belong.* Children tell a partner where they *belong* and what is there that shows that they *belong.* Share in a brief class discussion.

- Children draw where they *belong* (a bedroom, a house, a garden and so on), including some items that *belong* to them and that help them to feel that this is where they *belong.* Display the pictures.

- Teacher shows a photo of his/her family (or uses a familiar story book that illustrates a character and his or her family). Discuss *belonging* to a family with the class. Ask children to consider what happens in a family that shows that they *belong* (such as: we help each other, we eat together, we play together, we do things together, and we talk to each other).

- Teacher talks about other places where s/he *belongs*, such as the school. How does s/he know that s/he *belongs* there? (For instance: my chair is here, my books are here, the other teachers all know me, my class of children is here.) Children share in circle time or with partners where they *belong* and why they feel they *belong* there. (They will probably also use school as an example.)

- Children complete the drawing/writing frame (using the template in Figure 1.1: see CD. Teacher annotates it if required). Display the results.

---

### Questions to prompt discussion

- Where do you *belong*?
- What makes you feel you *belong*?
- Do you have things around you that *belong* to you?
- Does your family *belong* to you?
- Do you *belong* to your family?
- Do you think that you *belong* to anyone else?
- What makes you feel you *belong*?
- Do you *belong* anywhere else?
- Do you *belong* in this school?
- How do you know?
- Is there anything in the school that *belongs* to you? What?

Where do I belong?

I know I belong here because …

*Figure 1.1*

## Step 2 Apply

### How does belonging affect us and others?

● Teacher leads a class discussion to encourage the children to consider how they feel about *belonging* in different situations and in different circumstances.

**Questions to prompt discussion**

● Do you feel you *belong* everywhere you go?
● Are there some places you have been where you felt that you didn't *belong*? Where was that?
● How do you feel if you are in a place where you don't *belong*?
● Where do you feel you *belong* most?
● Is everyone the same?
● Do some people feel that they *belong* in different places? Why? Why not?

## *Step 3 Enquire*

### What is *belonging* about, and what helps people to feel they *belong*?

● Teacher tells the children that there is going to be a new member of the class (a teddy or a doll) and that she/he needs the children's ideas about what teddy/doll will need to make them feel he/she *belongs*.

The children might suggest:

● a school uniform
● a tray/drawer to keep things in
● a peg to hang his or her coat on
● a reading book bag
● a chair and a table to sit at
● some friends to help
● some friends to talk to and to play with
● his/her name in the register.

▶ ● Children sort cards (see Figure 1.2 and CD) and select the pictures that will help teddy/doll to feel that she/he *belongs*.

*Figure 1.2*

### *Step 4 Contextualise*

### What helps Christians to feel they belong in a church?

- Teacher could use a picture of a Christian child (see CD artwork A) or a persona doll (see information about persona dolls on page 6) to explore this aspect of the learning. Teacher explains that Joe (or other name) has a special place where he feels he *belongs*, called a church. Teacher asks, 'Shall we find out where Joe feels he *belongs*?'

    Taking the children on a visit to a church would be ideal here. Alternatively, explore aspects of a church through pictures (see CD).

    - Joe always sits with his mum. He feels he *belongs* in this seat.
    - Joe likes singing the songs. He knows all the words to the songs and this helps him feel he *belongs* (CD artwork 1).
    - In church all the people kneel on special cushions when they talk to God. Joe knows when to kneel down and when to stand up. This helps Joe feel he *belongs*.
    - Some of Joe's friends go to the church too. He feels he *belongs* with his friends.
    - The vicar knows Joe's name and that shows Joe that he *belongs.*
    - The vicar reads from the big book on a special stand at the front of the church. Everyone listens together. This helps them feel they *belong.*
    - Joe listens to special stories and draws pictures with the other children in a room at the back of the church. Some of his pictures are on the wall, and this helps him feel he *belongs* (CD artwork 2).
    - The stories that Joe hears are about someone called Jesus who lived a long time ago. Joe and all his friends and all the people in the church like to hear the stories about Jesus. Hearing the stories together helps Joe to feel he *belongs* (CD artwork 3).
- Invite a vicar or Sunday school teacher to share with the children some of the things that help Christians feel they *belong* (for instance: hear some Christian Sunday school songs, see some of the drawings that Christian children do, hear one of the stories that they like to hear, see some of the books and pictures that they look at).

### *Step 5 Evaluate*

### Is it important for Christians to feel they belong in a church?

- Teacher tells the story below, then talks about it with the class.

> ### Where does Joe belong?
>
> One Sunday Joe and his mum set off for church as usual, but this time they tried a short cut and went down a different road. They were a bit late so they rushed in without really looking.
>
> When they went in, things seemed to be different. There was no seat for them to sit on. Where was their usual seat?
>
> Joe and his mum looked around and there was nobody there that they knew. They could not see any of their friends. This was very peculiar.
>
> All the people started to sing, but they did not sing the songs that Joe and his mum knew, so they could not join in with the singing.
>
> After a while someone stood up to tell everyone a story, but this was not the vicar that Joe knew. It was someone Joe had never seen before. The story was not a story that Joe and his mum knew. This was really very odd indeed.
>
> Joe and his mum were very puzzled!

**Questions to prompt discussion**

- How do you think Joe felt?
- Did Joe and his mum *belong* in this place? Why? Why not?
- Do you think it is important to feel you *belong*? Why?
- Do you think Joe and his mum felt happy in this place or not?
- What do you think they ought to do?

- Teacher now tells the rest of the story, which provides a resolution.

After a little while a man came up and smiled at Joe and his mum.

'Are you new?' asked the smiling man.

'No,' said Joe's mum. 'We come here every Sunday, but everything is very different today. It feels odd.'

'Oh, you have come down the wrong road!' said the man. 'You want the church. It looks rather like this building on the outside. It is in the next road called Church Road.'

So Joe and his mum ran quickly along the next road, and there was their church. When they went in, their usual seat was empty. They could see their friends and they waved across the church. The vicar stood up and told a story, which was one of Joe's favourites, and then everyone sang a song. Joe loved the singing and he knew all the words. Now they knew that they were in the church where they belonged.

- Children draw pictures of Joe's face when he was in the place where he did not *belong* and then in the church where he did *belong* (see Figure 1.3 and CD). Children can play with a church jigsaw.

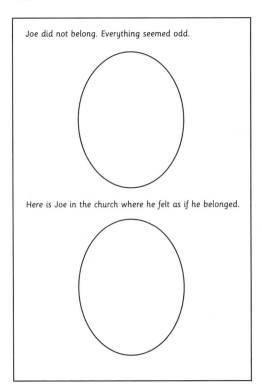

*Figure 1.3*

## Belonging in Buddhism

The children should explore Steps 1, 2 and 3 in the book (pages 10–12) before they engage with Steps 4 and 5 in this section.

### *Step 4 Contextualise*

### What helps Buddhists to feel they belong in a temple?

- Teacher could use a picture of a Buddhist child (see CD artwork B) or a persona doll  (see the information about persona dolls on page 6) to explore this aspect of the learning. Teacher explains that Elsa (or other name) has a special place where she feels she *belongs*, called a temple. Teacher asks, 'Shall we find out where Elsa feels she *belongs*?'

  Taking the children on a visit to a temple would be ideal here. Alternatively, explore aspects of a temple through pictures (see CD Artwork 4a and 4b).

  - ○ Elsa goes to the temple with her family. All the people leave their shoes at the door of the temple. Elsa knows that she *belongs* here because she knows where to leave her shoes and that her shoes will be safe. Everyone does the same thing.
  - ○ Elsa knows what to do when she comes to the temple. She goes up to the big statue of the Buddha. She likes looking at the statue because she feels it *belongs* to all of them and it makes her feel calm and quiet.
  - ○ Elsa bows her head and leaves some flowers in front of the statue. This is what everybody does. It shows that they all think the Buddha is very important.
  - ○ Elsa's mum and dad light a candle and some sticks which smell lovely. They know what to do because they *belong* here.
  - ○ After a while everyone sits on the floor. This is where they *belong*. All the people there are very calm and quiet together. Some people close their eyes. They all try to think kind thoughts.
  - ○ Sometimes Elsa comes to the temple with her friends. They go to a room in the temple with chairs and tables so that they can all learn about what the Buddha said. The children all feel that they *belong* because they are all learning together.
- Invite a Buddhist visitor to share with the children some of the things that help Buddhists feel they *belong* (for instance, show some pictures of the Buddha and light some incense sticks).

### *Step 5 Evaluate*

### Is it important for Buddhists to feel they belong in a temple?

- Teacher should continue to use the picture of the child or the persona doll for this area of learning. Set up the following scenario to stimulate children's ideas and responses.

> Elsa was fed up. It was the day when she and her family usually went to the temple to be with all their friends. They like being together with all the other Buddhists.
>
> Today they had to go to visit some people Elsa did not know. She felt very shy when she got to the house. They did not take their shoes off at the front door. When they got inside there were no statues of the Buddha and there were no flowers. There was some very loud music playing and people were shouting over the sound of the music. Elsa did not feel she belonged here at all.

- Discuss with the children what they think about Elsa's feelings.

---

**Questions to prompt discussion**

- Why do you think Elsa was so fed up?
- Did she feel she *belonged* in this house? Why? Why not?
- Would she feel happier if she had gone to the temple? Why? Why not?
- What difference would that make?
- Where do you think Elsa *belongs*?

---

- Children draw a picture of Elsa in the place where she *belongs*, or play with a Buddhist temple jigsaw.

## Belonging in Hinduism

The children should explore Steps 1, 2 and 3 in the book (pages 10–12) before they engage with Steps 4 and 5 in this section.

### *Step 4 Contextualise*

**What helps Hindus to feel they belong in a mandir?**

▶ ● Teacher could use a picture of a Hindu child (see CD artwork D) or a persona doll (see information about persona dolls on page 6) to explore this aspect of the learning. Teacher explains that Sita (or other name) has a special place where she feels she *belongs*, called a mandir. Teacher asks, 'Shall we find out where Sita feels she *belongs*?'

▶ Taking the children on a visit to a mandir would be ideal here. Alternatively, explore aspects of a mandir through pictures (see CD Artwork 5a).

- ○ At the door to the mandir all the people leave their shoes. Sita knows that she *belongs* here because she knows where to leave her shoes and that her shoes will be safe.
- ○ When they get inside they see the statue of Krishna. Krishna is very special to Sita and she loves to hear stories about him. She knows that she *belongs* here because she knows that the statue of Krishna is always here.
- ○ Sita knows what to do when she comes to the mandir. She goes up to Krishna and leaves some milk and some fruit. This is what everybody does.
- ○ Sita's mum and dad ring the bell in the mandir. They know that they should ring the bell because they *belong* here.
- ○ After a while everyone sits on the floor. Sita sits with her mum with all the other girls and ladies. This is where they *belong*. All the boys and men *belong* on the other side of the mandir.
- ○ Soon a lady starts playing a drum and a man plays some music and everyone starts to clap and sing. Sita knows the song and loves to sing along. They all know that they *belong* because they are all clapping and singing together. They are singing a song about Krishna.
- Invite a Hindu visitor to share with the children some of the things that help Hindus feel they *belong* (such as: hear some Hindu music, hear one of the stories that they like to hear, see some of the pictures that they look at).

### *Step 5 Evaluate*

### Is it important for Hindus to feel they belong in a mandir?

- The teacher should continue to use the picture of the child or the persona doll for this area of learning. Set up the following scenario to stimulate children's ideas and responses.

> Sita was a bit sad at the weekend. She had to go with her dad in the car to visit some people in another town. When they got there Sita got very bored because her friends were not there. She went into one of the rooms in the house but did not know if she should take her shoes off or not, so she went back to sit with her dad. She did not know what they were talking about, so she got more and more fed up. The trouble was that this was the day that she normally went to the mandir. She did not belong in this house with these people. She belonged in the mandir on a Saturday morning.

- Discuss with the children how they think Sita might have felt.

> ### Questions to prompt discussion
>
> - Why do you think Sita was so fed up?
> - Did she feel she *belonged* in this house? Why? Why not?
> - Would she feel happier if she had gone to the mandir? Why? Why not?
> - What difference would that make?
> - Where do you think Sita *belongs*?

- Children draw a picture of Sita in the place where she *belongs* or play with a mandir jigsaw.

## Belonging in Judaism

Children should explore Steps 1, 2 and 3 in the book (pages 10–12) before they engage with Steps 4 and 5 in this section.

### *Step 4 Contextualise*

### What helps Jews to feel they belong in a synagogue?

- Teacher could use a picture of a Jewish child (see CD artwork C) or a persona doll  (see the information about persona dolls on page 6) to explore this aspect of the learning. Teacher explains Joshua (or other name) has a special place where he feels he *belongs*, called a synagogue. Teacher asks, 'Shall we find out where Joshua feels he *belongs*?'

  Taking the children on a visit to a synagogue would be ideal here. Alternatively, explore aspects of a synagogue through pictures (see CD Artwork 6a and 6b).

  This particular example describes an orthodox synagogue.

- By the door to the synagogue is a special little box called a mezuzah. In the box is a special prayer. Joshua knows he belongs here because this little box is just like the one that he has on his doorpost at home.
- When Joshua and his family go into the synagogue, Joshua goes to some seats upstairs with the girls, little boys and their mums. He knows he *belongs* up here because he always sits in the same seat next to his friend. The men and some of the older boys *belong* in the seats downstairs.
- All the boys and men are wearing the same sort of special hats on their heads. This shows that they *belong* here.
- The curtains at the front of the synagogue are opened up and they can all see the special cupboard. The cupboard is opened and there are the Torah scrolls that belong to all the people. One of the men unrolls the scroll and sings out the words in a loud and clear voice.
- Joshua loves to hear the special words. He doesn't know what they mean yet because they are in a special language. Lots of the grown-ups know how to say the words because the special language *belongs* to them.

● Invite a Jewish visitor to share with the children some of the things that help Jews feel they *belong* (such as: hear some Jewish songs, hear one of the stories that they like to hear).

### Step 5 Evaluate

### Is it important for Jews to feel they belong in a synagogue?

● The teacher should continue to use the picture of the child or the persona doll for this area of learning. Set up the following scenario to stimulate children's ideas and responses.

> Poor Joshua was a bit fed up last Saturday. He went with his mum and dad and big brother to synagogue as usual. When they got there, there was no mezuzah on the door. 'This is strange,' said his dad. 'Do we belong here? There is no mezuzah to show that we belong here.'
>
> They went inside, but the way upstairs was shut. 'But we need to go upstairs. That is where we belong,' said Joshua to his mum.
>
> They were all very puzzled. They went in to see if the special cupboard was there, but they could not see it. There were big sheets over everything ... and a strong smell of paint.
>
> 'I don't like it here,' said Joshua. 'I don't feel we belong here.'

● Discuss with the children how they think Joshua might have felt.

### Questions to prompt discussion

- How do you think Joshua felt?
- Did Joshua and his family *belong* in this place? Why? Why not?
- Do you think it is important to feel you *belong*? Why? Why not?
- Do you think Joshua felt happy in this place or not?
- What do you think the family ought to do?

● Teacher now tells the rest of the story, which provides a resolution.

> Suddenly Joshua's mum started smiling. 'I remember now,' she said. 'Our synagogue is being painted. All our friends are meeting in another room in the synagogue.'
>
> One of the doors in the synagogue opened and they could see their friends. They could hear the special words being sung from the Torah scrolls. They knew that they were in the place where they belonged after all.

● Children draw a picture of Joshua in the place where he *belongs*, or play with a synagogue jigsaw.

## Belonging in Islam

Children should explore Steps 1, 2 and 3 in the book (pages 10–12) before they engage with Steps 4 and 5 in this section.

### *Step 4 Contextualise*

### What helps Muslims to feel they belong in a mosque?

● Teacher could use a picture of a Muslim child (see CD artwork E) or a persona doll (see the information about persona dolls on page 6) to explore this aspect of the learning. Teacher explains that Fatima (or other name) has a special place where she feels she *belongs*, called a mosque. Teacher asks, 'Shall we find out where Fatima feels she *belongs*?'

  Taking the children on a visit to a mosque would be ideal here. Alternatively, explore aspects of a mosque through pictures (see CD Artwork 7a, and 7b).

  ○ Fatima can hear the call to prayer. She and her family all go to the mosque where they *belong*. They know that this is where they *belong* when they all hear the call to prayer.

  ○ All the people leave their shoes at the door of the mosque. Fatima knows that she *belongs* here because she knows where to leave her shoes and that her shoes will be safe.

  ○ All the ladies and the girls are wearing scarves over their hair. Fatima knows that she *belongs* because she has her hair covered like them.

  ○ Fatima knows what to do when she comes to the mosque. She goes with her mother and auntie to a special washing place and washes her hands, her feet and her face. They are getting ready to speak to Allah (God). This is what everybody does.

  ○ The girls and the ladies *belong* in a special room to say their prayers. The boys and the men *belong* in their own special room for prayers.

  ○ They know that all the Muslims there *belong* together. They all stand and face the same way. They all listen to the prayers being said and they all make the same movements and get on their knees together because they all *belong* together.

  ○ Fatima and some of her friends go to the mosque during the week after school. They learn to write in a special way called Arabic. Fatima knows that she *belongs* in the mosque because all her friends learn to write and to say Arabic words.

- Invite a Muslim visitor to share with the children some of the things that help Muslims feel they *belong* (such as: hear the call to prayer, or show some Arabic words (see CD Artwork 7c) that Muslim children might learn to say or write).

### Step 5 Evaluate

### Is it important for Muslims to feel they belong in a mosque?

- The teacher should continue to use the picture of the child or the persona doll for this area of learning. Set up the following scenario to stimulate children's ideas and responses.

> Fatima was staying with her friend Cindy. One morning she went with Cindy and Cindy's mum and dad to a special meeting. It was in a big hall. Fatima felt very shy. She started to take her shoes off at the door, but Cindy said that she should keep her shoes on.
>
> Fatima was the only girl there who had a scarf covering her hair. She didn't feel she belonged there at all.
>
> All the men and women were sitting mixed up together and Fatima didn't know where to sit. She felt she didn't belong in any of the chairs. Cindy told Fatima to sit next to her. People got up and spoke, but Fatima didn't know when to stand and when to sit. She felt very strange.

- Discuss with the children how they think Fatima might have felt.

### Questions to prompt discussion

- How do you think Fatima felt?
- Do you think she feels she *belongs* in this hall with Cindy? Why? Why not?
- Do you think she wants to feel she *belongs*?
- What would make her feel she *belongs*?
- Is it important to feel you *belong* when you go somewhere?

- Children draw a picture of the place where Fatima *belongs*, or play with a mosque jigsaw.

### Belonging in Sikhism

Children should explore Steps 1, 2 and 3 in the book (pages 10–12) before they engage with Steps 4 and 5 in this section.

### Step 4 Contextualise

### What helps Sikhs to feel they belong in a gurdwara?

- Teacher could use a picture of a Sikh child (see CD artwork F) or a persona doll (see the information about persona dolls on page 6) to explore this aspect of the learning. Teacher explains that Amjid (or other name) has a special place where he feels he *belongs*, called a gurdwara. Teacher asks, 'Shall we find out where Amjid feels he *belongs*?'

Taking the children on a visit to a gurdwara would be ideal here. Alternatively, explore aspects of a gurdwara through pictures (see CD Artwork 8a and 8b).

○ All the people leave their shoes at the door to the gurdwara. Amjid knows he *belongs* here because he knows where to leave his shoes and that his shoes will be safe.

○ At the front of the large room there is a very special book called the Guru Granth Sahib. The book *belongs* here on the special platform.

○ Amjid knows he *belongs* here because he and his family and friends all know what to do. They go up in front of the special book and bow their heads to show that the book is very important.

○ Amjid knows he *belongs* here because he and lots of his friends have long hair. It is tied up on top of their heads with a piece of cloth around it, all the boys the same.

○ Everyone sits on the floor. Amjid sits with his dad and his brother, with all the other boys and men. This is where they *belong.* All the girls and women belong on the other side of the gurdwara.

○ Soon a woman starts playing a drum and a man plays some music and starts to sing. Amjid knows the song and loves to listen to the singing. They all know they *belong* because they are all clapping and listening together.

○ After a while everyone goes to another room. There is a delicious smell of food. Everyone gets some food and sits down to eat together. They know they *belong* here because they are all sharing the food and talking and laughing together.

● Invite a Sikh visitor to share with the children some of the things that help Sikhs feel they *belong* (such as: hear some Sikh songs, or share some special food in the class such as Indian sweets).

### *Step 5 Evaluate*

### Is it important for Sikhs to feel they *belong* in a gurdwara?

● The teacher should continue to use the picture of the child or the persona doll for this area of learning. Set up the following scenario to stimulate children's ideas and responses.

> Amjid says that his mum and dad got very cross with Amjid's brother the other day.
>
> Amjid's brother is 13 years old. He went to the hairdresser's and had all his long hair cut off without telling anyone.
>
> 'All Sikh boys have long hair,' said his mum when he got home. 'You will be the only Sikh boy at the gurdwara who has short hair. It will look as if you don't belong.'
>
> Amjid didn't know what to think or what to say, so he kept very quiet.

● Discuss with the children what they think about this scenario.

**Questions to prompt discussion**

- How do you think Amjid's brother felt?
- Do you think he will feel he *belongs* when he goes to the gurdwara? Why? Why not?
- Do you think Amjid should keep his hair long?
- Do you think that if he is the same as all the other boys, he will feel he *belongs*?
- Do you think he wants to feel he *belongs*?

- Children draw a picture of Amjid in the place where he *belongs*, or play with a gurdwara jigsaw.

## Resources on the CD

### *Figures*

1.1    Template – *Where do I belong?*
1.2    Cards – *Belonging*
1.3    Drawing frame – *Joe where he belongs/did not belong*

### *Artwork*

A.    Joe, a Christian boy
B.    Elsa, a Buddhist girl
C.    Joshua, a Jewish boy
D.    Sita, a Hindu girl
E.    Fatima, a Muslim girl
F.    Amjid, a Sikh boy
1.    Singing in Church
2.    Learning in Sunday School
3.    A reading from the Bible
4a.    Elsa's parents lighting a candle in the temple
4b.    A statue of Buddha
5a.    Sita in the mandir
6a.    Josh in the synagogue
6b.    The Torah scrolls in the Ark
7a.    Fatima and her mum doing ritual washing
7b.    Praying in the mosque
7c.    Arabic writing
8a.    Amjid in the gurdwara listening to a reading of the Guru Granth Sahib
8b.    Men and women listening to singing in the gurdwara

# Celebration

This concept (or key idea) is close to children's hearts. *Celebration* is an innate form of human expression, and this unit offers opportunities for children to encounter *celebrations* in religions alongside a growing understanding of their characteristics and the underlying significance of each one. The concept of *celebration* can form the foundation for exploring the concepts of *symbol*, *ritual* and *story*, *identity* and *community* later in Key Stage 2. This unit explores the concept of *celebration* within the context of how Christians *celebrate* Easter and also provides examples of how *celebration* can be explored within aspects of other major religions.

How do Buddhis*ts celebrate* Wesak?
How do Hindus *celebrate* Krishna's birthday?
How do Jews *celebrate* Hannukah?
How do Muslims *celebrate* Eid ul Fitr?
How do Sikhs *celebrate* Divali?

In this unit children start at the **enquire** element of learning to enable them to recognise what constitutes a *celebration*.

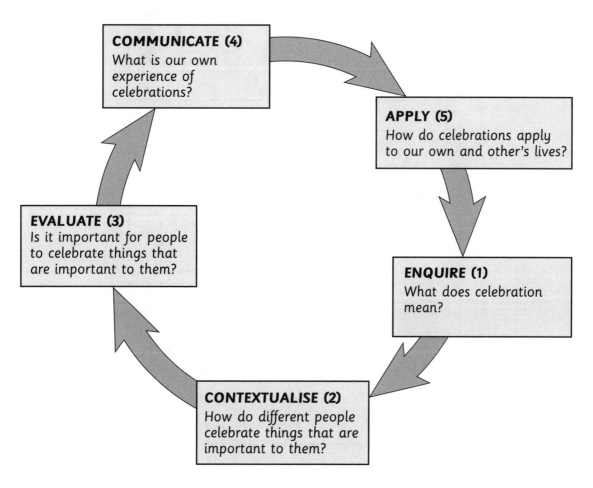

## Celebration in Christianity

### *Step 1 Enquire*

### What does *celebration* mean?

- Have a simple, non-religious *celebration* with the class: for example, the first day of summer, Teddy's birthday, New Goldfish Day, Granny Day.
- Ask the children to contribute their ideas about what is needed for a *celebration*, for instance:
  - friends and family
  - special food
  - cards
  - a song to sing
  - decorations
  - special clothes (or hats or badges)
  - something special to think about.
- Prepare and have the *celebration* with the children, noting that all the features of the *celebration* reflect what is being *celebrated.* The emphasis is that all these things are *reminders* of the focus of the *celebration.*
- Children select from the cards (see Figure 2.1 and CD) what is needed for a *celebration.*

*Figure 2.1*

### *Step 2 Contextualise*

#### How do Christians *celebrate* new life at Easter?

- Make a display of Easter cards, Easter decorations, Easter cakes, Easter gardens and so on.
- Teacher could use a picture of a Christian child (CD artwork A) or a persona doll (see  page 6), named Joe for example, to explore this aspect of learning, with reference to the display. The teacher says, 'I wonder how Joe *celebrates* new life at Easter. Shall we find out?'
  - Joe likes Easter morning because it is the start of the *celebration*. He gets to open his chocolate Easter eggs. They look lovely wrapped up in coloured foil.
  - For breakfast he has boiled eggs. He helps his mum to draw pictures of faces on everyone's egg. This is part of the *celebration.* They do it every Easter.
  - Joe's mum has put some decorations on the table to help them to *celebrate.* There are little fluffy chicks and some daffodils. They make everyone think of new life. Joe puts some Easter cards on the window sill.
  - Joe goes to the big building on Church Road. This is the church. Inside are lots of flowers and candles are lit. It looks lovely. Everyone in the church is *celebrating* too.
  - After church Joe goes to Sunday school with his friends in the room at the back of the church. They hear the story about Jesus dying and having a new life. They make a little garden in a tray and put flowers in it to remind them of new life (see CD artwork 9).
  - Joe joins in with the songs. They are about Jesus having a new life. Singing helps Joe feel as if he is *celebrating.*
  - When Joe gets home they have a special lunch and Granny comes too. The special lunch is part of the *celebration.*
  - In the afternoon they all have a piece of special Easter cake to *celebrate.* It has little Easter eggs made of sugar on the top.
- Teacher explains that when Joe and other Christians *celebrate* new life, they remember a special story. Tell the story below (also on CD).
- Ask a Sunday school teacher to visit the class to show the pupils some of the things Christian children do and make to *celebrate* Jesus' new life (such as eating chocolate eggs, making Easter cards, and decorating eggs).

---

#### Jesus has a new life

Many, many years ago there lived a man called Jesus. He was very kind and thoughtful and tried to help people. He used to travel around with his friends and he would tell people what God is like and how to be kind to each other.

He became quite famous and many people from miles around would go to hear Jesus tell his stories and to learn about God.

Other people got very worried about all the crowds gathering together to hear Jesus. They thought that he might cause trouble.

So something very sad happened. Jesus was put in prison for a short time and then he was killed and his body was put in a cave.

But that is not the end of the story. People who go to church, called Christians, say that after three days something amazing happened. Jesus' friends went to the cave and his dead body was not there. And then some of his friends saw Jesus walking around and perfectly well, and he told them that he had a new life.

So that is what Christians think about at Easter. They remember the story and celebrate Jesus having a new life.

### *Step 3 Evaluate*

### Is it important for Christians to *celebrate* new life at Easter?

● Through the picture of the Christian child or the Christian persona doll, ask the children to think about the new life *celebrations* they have explored.

> **Questions to prompt discussion**
>
> ● Do you think Joe likes the new life *celebrations*? Why? Why not?
> ● What do you think he likes best?
> ● What do you think helps him to remember Jesus' new life?
> ● If he did not have the new life *celebration*, do you think he would forget the story about Jesus' new life?
> ● Do you think it is important for Christians to have *celebrations* to remember Jesus' new life? Why? Why not?

● Teacher copies or duplicates and enlarges the three illustrated statements below, and places each statement on a separate table in the classroom.
● Teacher says, 'Joe likes the *celebrations* because they help him to think about Jesus' new life. What do you think is the best thing to help him to think about Jesus' new life? Choose one of the cards that will help Joe most.' (See Figure 2.2 and CD)

*Figure 2.2*

- Each child has one counter and must decide which statement they agree with most. The teacher will need to read each statement clearly and probably repeat it as children go around the tables and decide which statement they agree with most. They will need plenty of reassurance that there is no right answer. They can decide themselves where to put their counter.
- Teacher counts up the counters and shares the scores. She/he could encourage some further responses by comments such as:
  - This one got lots of counters. I wonder why.
  - This one only had two counters. Not many people agreed with this one. What do you think about that?

### *Step 4 Communicate*

### What is our own experience of *celebrations*?

- In circle time the teacher asks the children to close their eyes and think about a *celebration* they have had at home or with their family. The teacher can prompt with questions (see below).

---

**Questions to prompt children's thinking**

- Were there cards?
- Were there any presents?
- Were there any songs or music?
- Was there special food?
- Were there lots of people or only a few?
- What was the *celebration* for?
- Did they enjoy it? Why? Why not?

---

- Children open their eyes and tell a partner about the *celebration* they are thinking about.
- Share some of their examples with the class.
- Children draw pictures of the things that they had at their *celebrations* and label them (with support if necessary): for instance, friends and family, decorations, special food, singing, games, dancing, something special to think about. Some children may have photographs that they can display with their pictures. The teacher or a support assistant can annotate these with the children's responses to the question, 'What was your *celebration* for?'

### *Step 5 Apply*

### How do *celebrations* apply to our own and others' lives?

- Teacher continues from Step 4 to achieve continuity, and asks children the following questions to challenge their thinking.

**Questions to prompt discussion**

- Does everyone like *celebrating*? Why? Why not?
- Would you want to *celebrate* if you felt poorly? If the song was too noisy? If the sandwiches were horrible?
- Would you want to *celebrate* every day? Why? Why not?
- What other things do you *celebrate*?
- Why do you *celebrate* some things, but not others?
- Does everyone *celebrate* the same things? Why? Why not?

- The children complete the writing frame below (or the teacher or a support assistant annotates for the child). Place the responses on display with each child's picture (see Figure 2.3 and CD).

At my celebration I felt …

*Figure 2.3*

## Celebration in Buddhism

Children should explore Step 1 in the book (page 24) before they engage with Steps 2 and 3 in this section. This should then be followed by Steps 4 and 5 (pages 27–28).

### *Step 2 Contextualise*

### How do Buddhists *celebrate* Wesak?

- Teacher could use a picture of a Buddhist child (see CD artwork B) or a Buddhist  persona doll (see page 6), named Elsa for example, to explore this aspect of the learning. Teacher can say, 'I wonder how Elsa *celebrates* important things? Shall we find out?'
- Through the picture of the child or the persona doll the teacher can introduce some of the ways in which some Buddhists *celebrate* Wesak.
  - Elsa gets up early because it is a special *celebration.* It is Wesak. Elsa puts on new clothes and goes to the big building called the temple with her mum and dad.
  - Elsa and her family take some food with them. Everyone is giving food to the men who live at the temple (monks) so that they can share in the *celebrations* and remember the Buddha.
  - Elsa has also brought some flowers with her. When they are in the temple she bows her head and thinks about the Buddha, then she puts the flowers by the statue of the Buddha (see CD artwork 11).
  - Everyone in the temple sits on the floor. They all sing together as part of the *celebration*. Elsa thinks singing is a really good way to *celebrate.*
  - When Elsa's family goes home there are lots of cards to open. They have pictures of flowers and the Buddha on them. She puts them on the shelf as a decoration for the *celebrations.*
  - In the afternoon Elsa's granny spends time reading her some stories about the Buddha. This is a special treat for the Wesak *celebrations*.
  - In the evening is the most exciting part of the *celebrations*. Lots of families light lamps to help them to *celebrate* and remember the Buddha. The town looks lovely lit up with lamps.
- The teacher tells the story (below and on CD) about the enlightenment of the Buddha.
- The children can make some cards to give to Elsa to help her *celebrate* Wesak.
- Teacher can set up a simple Buddhist shrine in the classroom like the one that Elsa puts flowers on at the Wesak *celebrations.*

### The Buddha understands all about life

Many years ago lived a prince called Siddhartha. He was good and kind and very clever, but he was never allowed out of the palace. His father wanted to keep him safe. All his life Prince Siddhartha stayed in the palace. He was very happy and had all he wanted.

When Prince Siddhartha grew up he became very curious about the world outside the palace. One night he decided to creep out of the palace to see what it was like.

The Prince saw three things that really made him think. First of all, Prince Siddhartha saw a person who was very ill and lying down. This made Siddhartha very sad. 'I didn't know that people could get ill,' he said.

A little further on he saw someone who was very old. The man could not walk very well and he struggled along with the help of a stick. This also made Siddhartha sad. 'I did not know that people could get old,' he said.

The next person Siddhartha saw made him very sad indeed. Siddhartha saw someone who had died. 'I did not know that people could die,' he said.

He went back to the palace feeling very upset. He did not know that people could suffer so much. Siddhartha thought and thought about the things he had seen. He could not work out why life can be so sad.

One night Siddhartha left the palace and went to live on his own in the woods. He kept on thinking and trying to work out how people could feel at peace. He wore rags, he didn't eat much food, but he kept on thinking and thinking, for ages and ages ... for years and years.

One day Siddhartha was sitting under a tree, thinking, when suddenly his mind was clear. 'I understand now,' he said. 'I know how people can feel at peace.'

From then on the prince told everyone about how they could feel at peace. All the people called him the Buddha, which means great teacher.

### Questions to prompt discussion

- Do you think Elsa and other Buddhists like to hear this story as part of the *celebrations*? Why?
- Which part of the *celebrations* do you think Elsa likes most? Why?
- What does Elsa remember about the Buddha when she is *celebrating* with her friends and family?

### *Step 3 Evaluate*

**Is it important for Buddhists to *celebrate* Wesak?**
- Teacher should continue to use the picture of the Buddhist child or the persona doll for this area of learning.
- Teacher copies or duplicates and enlarges the three illustrated statements below and places the statements on each table in the classroom.
- Teacher then says to the children, 'Elsa likes the *celebrations* because they help her to think about the Buddha. What do you think is the best thing to help her to think about the Buddha? Choose one of the cards that will help Elsa most.' (See Figure 2.4 and CD)

Putting flowers in front of the Buddha statue

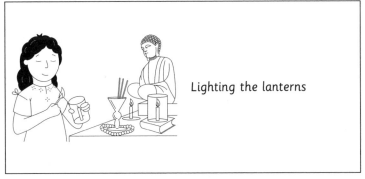

Lighting the lanterns

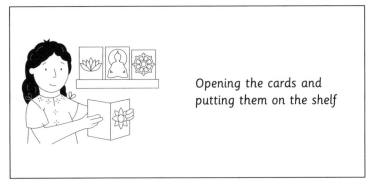

Opening the cards and putting them on the shelf

*Figure 2.4*

● Each child points out or places a counter on the card they have chosen. The teacher encourages them to say why they have chosen that card. There are no right or wrong answers here, but children should be encouraged to express their own ideas.

**Questions to prompt discussion**

- Do you think Elsa likes to *celebrate*? Why? Why not?
- Do you think she would like to *celebrate* Wesak every day? Why? Why not?
- Could Elsa join in the *celebrations* and forget all about the Buddha?
- Would it matter if Elsa forgot to think about the Buddha at the *celebrations*? Why? Why not?
- Does everyone at the *celebrations* like to think about the Buddha, do you think?
- What are the *celebrations* for?

Return to page 27 to Steps 4 and 5, to complete the cycle of learning.

## Celebration in Hinduism

Children should explore Step 1 in the book (page 24) before they engage with Steps 2 and 3 in this section. This should then be followed by Steps 4 and 5 (pages 27–28).

### *Step 2 Contextualise*

### How do Hindus *celebrate* Krishna's birthday?

- The teacher could use a picture of a Hindu child (CD artwork D) or a Hindu persona doll (see page 6) called Sita, for example, to explore this aspect of the learning. Teacher says, 'I wonder how Sita *celebrates* important things. Shall we find out?'

  Through the picture of the child or the persona doll the teacher can introduce some of the ways in which some Hindus *celebrate* Krishna's birthday.

  - ○ Sita is allowed to stay up very, very late because it is a special *celebration*. It is Krishna's birthday. In the front room is a shrine. Sita's mum has been getting it ready for the *celebrations*. It is a special little table with statues on it and little lights and pictures and models of Krishna.

  - ○ Sita and all her family get ready to *celebrate*. They wash and put on their best clothes. At midnight they all go to look at the shrine. Sita puts some special sweets on the shrine and her brother puts some milk there (see CD artwork 13). These are gifts for Krishna. The little lights are lit and the perfume sticks make the room smell lovely. On the shrine is a little cot with a model of baby Krishna in it. They sing special songs about baby Krishna and the night he was born.

  - ○ The next day Sita and her family go to the temple. Sita's dad has some coconuts to put by the big shrine at the temple and her mum has some more milk to put there. They put them in front of the statue of Krishna to show that they are thinking about him at his birthday *celebrations*. They say prayers to Krishna.

  - ○ Everyone in the temple sits on the floor. They all sing together as part of the *celebration*. Sita thinks singing is a really good way to *celebrate*.

  - ○ When the family goes home Sita opens some of the cards. They have pictures of flowers and Krishna on them. She puts them on the shelf as a decoration for the *celebrations*.

  - ○ Sita's family and friends have a huge meal as part of the *celebrations*. There is so much special food that Sita feels really full up. In the afternoon Sita's auntie spends time reading her the story about when Krishna was born. She loves this story.

- Teacher tells the children the story Sita hears as part of the *celebrations* (see below and CD).

- The children can make some cards to give to Sita to help her *celebrate* Krishna's birthday.

- The teacher can set up a simple Hindu shrine in the classroom like the one that Sita has in her home.

## Krishna is born

Many, many years ago, in a land far away, lived a very wicked, mean, horrible king called Kamsa. He was so mean and horrible that all the people in his land were very scared of him and hated him.

One day the wicked king Kamsa called for a fortune-teller to tell him what would happen in his life. The fortune-teller knew what was going to happen.

'A baby will be born, O King, and he will grow up to take over your kingdom. He will become King.'

Kamsa was furious. 'How can this happen?' he shouted. 'Who is going to have this baby?'

'Well, Sire, your sister will have the special baby.'

Kamsa was so cross that he ordered his soldiers to go and get his sister, and her husband, and throw them into prison.

Well, they had a really miserable time in prison. They could not go out, or see the sunshine, or eat nice food. And what was most awful was that each time they did have a baby, wicked Kamsa came and took their baby away from them. They were so sad.

One night, however, something amazing happened. There was a bright moon and outside the prison all the flowers were out. A lovely smell of flowers drifted into the prison. On that special night baby Krishna was born. He was the most beautiful baby imaginable and Krishna's mother and father loved him dearly.

'How can we save him?' whispered Krishna's mother. 'What shall we do to stop that mean king Kamsa taking him away?'

Krishna's father quickly picked up some rags from the floor and wrapped up the tiny baby Krishna and put him in a basket. And carrying baby Krishna in the basket under his arm, he headed straight for the door.

'But the door is locked!' exclaimed his wife. But as Krishna's father got to the door, the key turned, the bolts slid open, the chains fell off and the door quietly creaked open.

'Watch out for the guards!' whispered Krishna's mother. But Krishna's father crept past all the guards, who stayed fast asleep.

Now he was at the great big gates to the prison. They were huge and had big locks on them and huge chains and bolts. But as Krishna's father got closer, the chains fell to the ground, the keys turned in the locks and the bolts slid open. The gates opened, all on their own, with just the right amount of space for Krishna's father to squeeze through carrying baby Krishna.

Now they were free. On and on ran Krishna's father, through the fields and over the hills and through the woods until, at last, he came to a great river. On the other side of the river was a different land. The other side of the river was outside the wicked king Kamsa's kingdom. They were nearly safe!

Into the river waded Krishna's father carrying baby Krishna in the basket. The water was calm, but as they got towards the middle of the river it started to become very rough and the waves got higher and higher. Now Krishna's father was really worried. He held baby Krishna in the basket above his head as the waves battered him and nearly pushed him over.

Then something amazing happened. Baby Krishna looked down from the basket and dipped his tiny toe into the raging river. Instantly, the water calmed down and there was a pathway in the water to allow Krishna's father to walk safely to the other side.

Krishna's father had some friends who lived on this side of the river. They were good, kind people, so Krishna's father knocked on their door.

He told them about the wicked Kamsa and about the beautiful baby Krishna being in danger. 'Will you look after him for us?' asked Krishna's father.

'Yes, we will,' they answered. And they did. They loved Krishna and cared for him all his life.

Krishna grew up to be a good, brave, kind and wonderful prince. And do you know? He did take over the kingdom of the wicked king Kamsa and everybody loved him.

### Step 3 Evaluate

### Is it important for Hindus to *celebrate* Krishna's birthday?

- Teacher should continue to use the picture of the Hindu child or the persona doll for this area of learning.
- Teacher copies or duplicates and enlarges the three illustrated statements below and places the statements on each table in the classroom.
- The teacher says to the children, 'Sita likes the *celebrations* because they help her to think about Krishna. What do you think is the best thing to help her to think about Krishna? Choose one of the cards that will help Sita most.' (see Figure 2.5 and CD)

Figure 2.5

- The children point to or place a counter on the card that they have chosen. Teacher encourages them to say why they have chosen that card. There are no right or wrong answers here, but children should be encouraged to express their own ideas.

---

**Questions to prompt discussion**

- Do you think Sita likes to *celebrate*? Why? Why not?
- Do you think she would like to *celebrate* Krishna's birthday every day? Why? Why not?
- Could Sita join in the *celebrations* and forget all about Krishna?
- Would it matter if Sita forgot to think about Krishna at the *celebrations*? Why? Why not?
- Does everyone at the *celebrations* like to think about Krishna, do you think?
- What are the *celebrations* for?

---

Return to page 27 to Steps 4 and 5, to complete the cycle of learning.

## Celebration in Judaism

Children should explore Step 1 in the book (page 24) before they engage with Steps 2 and 3 in this section. This should then be followed by Steps 4 and 5 in the book (pages 27–28).

### Step 2 Cotextualise

### How do Jews *celebrate* Hannukah?

- Teacher could use a picture of a Jewish child (see CD artwork C) or a Jewish persona  doll (see page 6) called Joshua, for example, to explore this aspect of the learning. Teacher says, 'I wonder how Joshua *celebrates* important things? Shall we find out?'
  Through the picture of the child or the doll the teacher can introduce some of the ways in which some Jews *celebrate* Hannukah.
  - ○ Joshua likes to *celebrate* Hannukah. The *celebration* lasts for over a week! Yesterday his mum polished the special candleholder called a *menorah* which takes eight candles (and one extra to light the others with). Today is the first day, and Joshua gets to help his sister to light the first candle. Candles help him feel that this is a special *celebration* (see CD artwork 15).
  - ○ They have lots of cards around the room wishing them all a happy Hannukah. Joshua made a card to send to his mum and dad and he drew a picture of the candlestick on the front with all the candles lit.
  - ○ Joshua loves the special food that they all eat at Hannukah. Tonight they will have latkes. These are special fried potato cakes. Tomorrow his mum says that she will make doughnuts. The special food really helps Joshua's family *celebrate* well.
  - ○ When Joshua and his family have finished eating the special food they sing Hannukah songs and remember the old story of God making something amazing happen. They also play dreidels. This is a really fun game when they spin a little plastic spinning top. Joshua often wins lots of sweets when he plays dreidels.

○ Joshua's family all go to the synagogue during the *celebrations*. This is a big building where they meet with their Jewish friends and family. They listen to prayers and think about the special story when God made something amazing happen.

- Teacher tells the story that Joshua hears as part of the *celebrations* at Hannukah (see below and CD).
- Children make a Hannukah card that Joshua could send to his friends.
- Make latkes or doughnuts with the children to share with Joshua.
- Learn a Hannukah song to sing to Joshua.
- Light the Hannukah menorah each day of the school week.

### God made something amazing happen

Many, many hundreds of years ago lived some people who were Jews. But they were not happy people. They were very unhappy because some soldiers had attacked their country and brought in strange people who started living in their land. The Jews couldn't do any of the things they wanted to. They could not even go to their special temple to pray to God. In fact, the soldiers and the people who lived in their land went into the temple and spoiled it all and made it dirty. It was horrible!

There was a very brave Jew called Judah the Maccabee, and he and some other Jews went off into the hills to plan how they could get their country back. They needed to be strong and brave so that they could fight the soldiers and get them to leave. So, every now and again, Judah the Maccabee would lead the other Jews out of the hills to fight the soldiers.

Gradually, a little bit at a time, Judah the Maccabee and the other Jews fought the soldiers until they all left. Now the Jews had their land back again.

The next thing to do was to clean up their temple. They scrubbed and cleaned the temple from top to bottom until they felt that it was ready to go into and pray to God. But one thing was missing. They had a special oil lamp which they had to light to make the temple really special for God. The trouble was, there was only a tiny drop of oil left, only enough to light the lamp for a very little while. And it would take a long time to get any more oil.

So what the Jews did was light the little bit of oil in the lamp anyway. Do you know what? A truly amazing thing happened. The lamp stayed alight for one day, for two days, for three days, for four days, for five days, for six days, for seven days, and for eight days. The little bit of oil never ran out for all that time and the lamp kept burning for eight whole days. God had made a truly amazing thing happen and the light kept on burning.

### Step 3 Evaluate

### Is it important for Jews to *celebrate* Hannukah?

- The teacher should continue to use the picture of the child or the persona doll for this area of learning.
- Teacher copies or duplicates and enlarges the three illustrated statements below (and on CD) and places the statements on each table in the classroom.
- Teacher tells the children, 'Joshua likes the *celebrations* because they help him to think about how God made the light stay burning. What do you think is the best thing to help him to think about the story? Choose one of the cards that will help Joshua most.' (See Figure 2.6 and the CD)

*Figure 2.6*

● Each child points to or places a counter on the card they have chosen. The teacher encourages them to say why they have chosen that card. There are no right or wrong answers here, but children should be encouraged to express their own ideas.

**Questions to prompt discussion**

● Do you think Joshua likes to *celebrate*? Why? Why not?
● Do you think he would like to *celebrate* every day? Why? Why not?
● Could Joshua join in the *celebrations* and forget all about how God helped?
● Would it matter if Joshua forgot to think about God at the *celebrations*? Why? Why not?
● Does everyone at the *celebrations* like to think about God, do you think?
● What are the *celebrations* for?

Return to page 27 to Steps 4 and 5, to complete the cycle of learning.

## Celebration in Islam

Children should explore Step 1 in the book (page 24) before they engage with Steps 2 and 3 in this section. This should then be followed by Steps 4 and 5 in the book (pages 27–28).

### *Step 2 Contextualise*

### How do Muslims *celebrate* Eid ul Fitr?

- Teacher could use a picture of a Muslim child (see CD artwork E) or a Muslim persona doll (see page 6), called Fatima, for example, to explore this aspect of the learning. The teacher says, 'I wonder how Fatima *celebrates* important things. Shall we find out?'

    Through the picture of the child or the doll the teacher can introduce some of the ways in which some Muslims *celebrate* Eid ul Fitr.

    - Today is Eid. Fatima loves this *celebration*. She gets up early, has a wash and puts on brand new clothes. All her family do the same thing. They all look very smart in their best new clothes.
    - Fatima and her family go together to the big building down the road called the mosque. She can tell that this is a special *celebration* today. There are hundreds of people here. Everyone is hugging or shaking hands and saying 'Eid Mubarak'.
    - When they are in the mosque, Fatima goes with her mother and the other women and girls to a large room. They all face the same way and kneel down together, and bow down together when they are saying their prayers. This is a special time when they are all thinking about Allah (God). This is what the *celebration* is for.
    - When they are in the mosque they put some money in a box. This goes to help poor people so that everyone can enjoy the *celebration*. Fatima puts some of her pocket money in the box.
    - When Fatima goes home she helps to open some of the cards. They all say 'Eid Mubarak'. They have flowers and birds on them and special writing. Fatima puts the cards on the shelf because it is a special *celebration* (see CD artwork 17).
    - All the grown-ups have not been eating during the day for a whole month. They do this to help them to concentrate on Allah (God). Today is the *celebration* when they can eat as much as they like. There is so much lovely food for this *celebration*. Fatima helps her mother to put the food out for her father, her brothers and her uncles. Fatima eats her special food with her mother, her aunties and her girl cousins in another room. The food is lovely. They all laugh and chat.
    - Some of Fatima's cousins have brought some sweets for Fatima as a special present for the *celebration.*
- Children make an Eid card that Fatima could send to her friends.
- Make special sweets with the children to share with Fatima.

### *Step 3 Evaluate*

### Is it important for Muslims to *celebrate* Eid ul Fitr?

- The teacher should continue to use the picture of the Muslim child or the persona doll for this area of learning.
- Teacher copies or duplicates and enlarges the three illustrated statements below and places the statements on each table in the classroom.
- The teacher says to the children, 'Fatima likes the *celebrations* because they help her to think about Allah (God). What do you think is the best thing to help her to think about Allah? Choose one of the cards that will help Fatima most.' (See Figure 2.7 and CD)

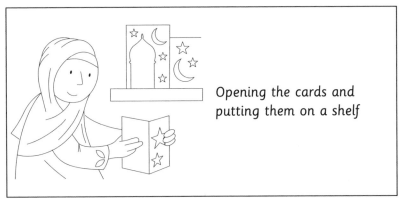

Eating the lovely food

Going to the mosque and saying prayers with her mum

Opening the cards and putting them on a shelf

*Figure 2.7*

● Each child points to or places a counter on the card they have chosen. The teacher encourages them to say why they have chosen that card. There are no right or wrong answers here, but children should be encouraged to express their own ideas.

**Questions to prompt discussion**

● Do you think Fatima likes to *celebrate*? Why? Why not?
● Do you think she would like to *celebrate* every day? Why? Why not?
● Could Fatima join in the *celebrations* and forget all about Allah (God)?
● Would it matter if Fatima forgot to think about Allah at the *celebrations*? Why? Why not?
● Does everyone at the *celebrations* like to think about Allah, do you think?
● What are the *celebrations* for?

Return to page 27 to Steps 4 and 5, to complete the cycle of learning.

## Celebration in Sikhism

Pupils should explore Step 1, in the book (page 24) before they engage with Steps 2 and 3 in this section. This should then be followed by Steps 4 and 5 in the book (pages 27–28).

### *Step 2 Contextualise*

#### How do Sikhs *celebrate* Divali?

- ▶ The teacher could use a picture of a Sikh child (See CD artwork F) or a Sikh persona doll (see page 6), called Amjid, for example, to explore this aspect of the learning. The teacher says, 'I wonder how Amjid (or other name) *celebrates* important things. Shall we find out?'

  Through the picture of the child or the doll the teacher can introduce some of the ways in which some Sikhs *celebrate* Divali.

  - ○ Amjid is excited today because it is the day for Divali *celebrations*. His mum and dad have given him some sweets.
  - ○ Later on Amjid and his family go to the big building in town called the gurdwara. He sees some of his friends here with their families. All his friends are excited about the *celebrations* too. They tell each other what sweets they had.
  - ○ Everyone in the gurdwara sits on the floor. They all listen to the singing as part of the *celebration*. Amjid thinks singing is a really good way to *celebrate* (see CD artwork 19).
  - ○ When they are in the gurdwara someone stands up and tells the story about Guru Hargobind. Amjid loves to hear this story at Divali time. It is what the *celebrations* are for.
  - ○ Everyone in the gurdwara goes to another room to share food together. Amjid sits with his friends. After the main meal there are more special sweets to eat. His mum tells him that if he eats too many he will feel sick.
  - ○ Amjid really enjoys the evening of Divali *celebrations*. He helps his mum to light little lamps in the house. It looks lovely. Amjid thinks that lighting lamps is a good way to *celebrate*.
  - ○ Amjid and his family go out later to see a big firework display. The rockets are fantastic. What a good way to *celebrate*.
- ▶ Tell the children the story that Amjid hears at the gurdwara as part of the *celebrations* (see below and on CD).
- Make some Divali sweets with the children to share with Amjid.
- Children paint some pictures of the fireworks that Amjid sees at the *celebrations*.

### Guru Hargobind is released from prison

The Sikh people had a great leader called Guru Hargobind. A guru is a great teacher who can help people to understand God and teach them how God wants them to behave. But Guru Hargobind had been taken away. He had been arrested by the emperor of the land at that time and thrown into prison.

Poor Hargobind had done nothing wrong. He was a good man and all he had done was to talk to the Sikh people and help them to be good Sikhs and to do their duty to God. But the emperor was worried about Hargobind. Lots of people listened to Hargobind and did as he told them, and the emperor thought that maybe Hargobind was just a bit too powerful.

This is what the emperor always did when he thought someone might be getting more powerful than he was. In fact, it had happened to 52 Indian princes as well. The emperor had been worried about their power and thrown them into prison too.

Luckily, Hargobind had friends who knew the emperor. They gradually persuaded the emperor to change his mind and tell Hargobind that he would be released from prison.

'You can go. You are free,' announced the emperor.

'Well, thank you,' answered Hargobind, 'but I will only go if the 52 princes are also released.'

Well, this was a blow to the emperor. He didn't expect to have to release all the prisoners, so he went away and thought about it. He thought he would be very clever. He went back to Hargobind and announced, 'You can take some of the princes with you when you leave, but only as many as can hold on to your coat when you go.' He thought that no more than three or four men could hold on to someone's coat.

Now, Guru Hargobind was very clever indeed. He arranged for a coat to be made for him which had 52 tassels hanging from it. When the day of his release came, down the passageway walked Guru Hargobind, followed by all the 52 princes who each had hold of a tassel attached to Hargobind's coat. There was nothing the emperor could do. They were all released from prison.

All the Sikh people were delighted and celebrated the release of their great Guru. When he arrived at the great Temple in Amritsar, it was decorated with lights to celebrate Hargobind's freedom.

## Step 3 Evaluate

### Is it important for Sikhs to *celebrate* Divali?

- The teacher should continue to use the picture of the Sikh child or the persona doll for this area of learning.
- Teacher copies or duplicates and enlarges the three illustrated statements below and places the statements on each table in the classroom.
- The teacher says to the children, 'Amjid likes the *celebrations* because they help him to think about Guru Hargobind. What do you think is the best thing to help him to think about the Guru? Choose one of the cards that will help Amjid most.' (see Figure 2.8 and CD)

Eating the lovely sweets

Listening to the singing in the gurdwara

Seeing the fireworks

*Figure 2.8*

● Each child points to or places a counter on the card they have chosen. The teacher encourages them to say why they have chosen that card. There are no right or wrong answers here, but children should be encouraged to express their own ideas.

**Questions to prompt discussion**

● Do you think Amjid likes to *celebrate*? Why? Why not?
● Do you think he would like to *celebrate* Divali every day? Why? Why not?
● Could Amjid join in the *celebrations* and forget all about Guru Hargobind?
● Would it matter if Amjid forgot to think about Guru Hargobind at the *celebrations*? Why? Why not?
● Does everyone at the *celebrations* like to think about Hargobind, do you think?
● What are the *celebrations* for?

Return to page 27 to Steps 4 and 5, to complete the cycle of learning.

## Resources on the CD

### *Figures*

2.1   Cards – *Celebration*
2.2   Cards – helping Joe think about Jesus' new life
2.3   Writing frame – *At my celebration I felt*
2.4   Cards – helping Elsa think about the Buddha
2.5   Cards – helping Sita think about Krishna
2.6   Cards – helping Josh think about how God made the light stay burning
2.7   Cards – helping Fatima think about Allah
2.8   Cards – helping Amjid think about Guru Hargobind

### *Artwork*

A.   Joe, a Christian boy
B.   Elsa, a Buddhist girl
C.   Joshua, a Jewish boy
D.   Sita, a Hindu girl
E.   Fatima, a Muslim girl
F.   Amjid, a Sikh boy
9.   Joe making an Easter garden
11.  Elsa placing flowers by the statue of the Buddha
13.  Sita places sweets on her shrine for Krishna
15.  Josh helps his sister light the menorah
17.  Fatima putting up Eid cards
19.  Amjid listening to singing in the gurdwara

### *Stories: Christian*

*Jesus has a new life*

### *Stories: Buddhist*

*The Buddha understands all about life*

### *Stories: Hindu*

*Krishna is born*

### *Stories: Jewish*

*God made something amazing happen*

### *Stories: Sikh*

*Guru Hargobind is released from prison*

# Remembering

The concept or key idea of *remembering* has enormous potential as it can be applied to many religious practices. It is particularly helpful for young children to recognise the different ways in which religious people *remember* events, people and stories because they are precious and meaningful to them and they wish to preserve them and keep them alive. The concept of *remembering* can form the foundation for exploring symbol, ritual and myth later in Key Stage 2. This unit explores the concept of *remembering* in the context of how Christians *remember* Jesus at Christmas. It also provides examples of how *remembering* can be explored within aspects of other major religions in relation to festivals, stories or people.

How do Buddhists *remember* the Buddha?
How do Hindus *remember* Lord Vishnu at Holi?
How do Jews *remember* God's help at Passover?
How do Muslims *remember* the story about the angel's message for Muhammad (pbuh)?
How do Sikhs *remember* Guru Nanak?

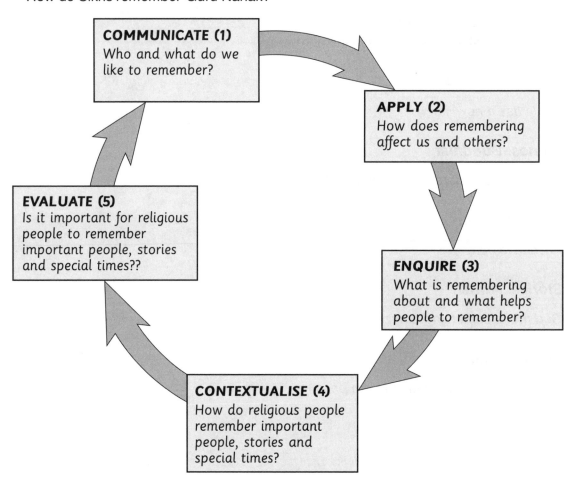

**COMMUNICATE (1)**
Who and what do we like to remember?

**APPLY (2)**
How does remembering affect us and others?

**ENQUIRE (3)**
What is remembering about and what helps people to remember?

**CONTEXTUALISE (4)**
How do religious people remember important people, stories and special times?

**EVALUATE (5)**
Is it important for religious people to remember important people, stories and special times??

## Remembering in Christianity

### *Step 1 Communicate*

#### Who and what do we like to *remember*?

- Teacher shows a photograph of someone she/he likes to *remember*, and asks the children to think about and suggest why that might be (for instance, 'You love them', 'They live a long way away and you don't see them much', 'They help you', 'They make you laugh').
- Teacher asks the children to close their eyes and think about somebody they like to *remember.* Allow a few moments for the children to reflect quietly.
- Children share their ideas with a partner.
- In class discussion the teacher asks the children why they like to *remember* that person.

---

**Questions to prompt discussion**

- Who do you like to *remember*?
- Why do you like to *remember* them?
- Are there quite a few people you like to *remember*?
- Why do you like to *remember* them?
- Do you *remember* different people for different reasons?
- Are there some people you wish you could *remember* more about? Who? Why?
- Are there some people that you wish you could forget? Who? Why?

---

- Teacher now asks the children about other things they *remember*, such as things that have happened (holidays, parties, celebrations) or stories they have heard.
- Children share with a partner an event or/and a story they *remember*. Note: the teacher may wish to deal with events and stories separately to avoid confusion.
- Children complete one or more of the writing and drawing frames below. (See Figure 3.1, 3.1a, 3.1b and CD)

---

**Questions to prompt discussion**

- What do you *remember*?
- Why do you *remember*?
- Do you *remember* some events or stories more than others? Why?
- Are there some events or stories you would like to *remember* more about? Why?
- Are there some events or stories you would like to forget? Why?

---

This is someone I remember.

I remember them because ...

Figure 3.1

This is a story I remember.

I remember it because ...

Figure 3.1a

This is something that happened that I remember.

I remember it because …

*Figure 3.1b*

## *Step 2 Apply*

### How does *remembering* affect us and others?

- Teacher should encourage the children to share some of the people, stories and events they *remember* by showing some of the completed writing and drawing frames. The children can role play some of the events and tell the others why they *remember* them, or tell the class the story they *remember*, or talk about the person they *remember*.
- Teacher leads a class discussion about how *remember*ing can affect us all in different ways.

### Questions to prompt discussion

- Does everyone *remember* the same things? Why? Why not?
- Are any of the things you *remember* the same as others?
- Is it easier to *remember* some things more than others? Why?
- Is *remembering* a good thing? Why? Why not?
- Do you think *remembering* makes people happy or sad?
- Is it important to *remember*? Why? Why not?
- Is it possible to *remember* everyone, everything and every story?
- Why do you think we *remember* some things more than others?
- Are there some things we would rather not *remember*? Why?
- How do you feel when you *remember* things and people?

### *Step 3 Enquire*

**What is *remembering* about, and what helps people to remember?**

- Children work in small groups with the teacher or a support assistant. The children offer their suggestions, brainstorming their ideas about what helps us *remember*. Teacher or support assistant scribes. What helps the children to *remember*:
  - a person (children might say, for example, a photograph, a letter, a card, a telephone call, a visit from the person, someone telling them about the person)
  - a story (children might say, for example, seeing the pictures/illustrations, hearing the story again, reading the story, someone telling them about the story, going over the story in your mind, someone asking about it)
  - something that has happened (children might say, for example, a recording on a video camera or picture on a mobile phone, someone talking about what happened, photographs, seeing the people who were there with you, eating the same food, hearing the same music, thinking about it in your head).
- Teacher can share the different group responses and collate them as a list for display to refer to later in the unit of work.
- Teacher should ask the children: 'Do you know more about *remembering* now than you did before? Has anyone said something that surprised you or made you think? What was that?'

### *Step 4 Contextualise*

**How do Christians *remember* Jesus at Christmas?**

- ▶ Teacher could use a picture of a Christian child (see CD artwork A) or a Christian persona doll (see page 6), called Joe (or other name), to explore this aspect of the learning. Teacher might say, 'You *remember* that Joe (or other name) is a Christian. He has someone he likes to *remember* at Christmas time. He *remember*s Jesus and the stories about when he was born.'

  Teacher should continue to use the picture of the child or the persona doll to explore how Christians *remember* Jesus.
- ▶ Show the children a variety of Christmas cards with the image of baby Jesus in the manger, or show the images provided (see CD artwork 21a–d) on the whiteboard.

> **Questions to prompt discussion**
>
> - What do you notice about these pictures?
> - What do you notice about Jesus?
> - What do you think about all the other people in the pictures?
> - Why do you think they are there?
> - Do you think these pictures might help Joe to *remember* baby Jesus? Why? Why not?

- ▶ Teacher tells the story of the birth of Jesus (see below and CD) that Joe and other Christians like to *remember*.

### The story of the birth of baby Jesus

A long, long time ago there lived a young woman called Mary. One day she had a huge surprise. In the middle of the room was a very bright light and in the middle of the bright light was a person. It was an angel. Mary was terrified.

'Do not be afraid,' said the angel. 'I have some good news for you.' The angel told Mary that God had chosen her to have a very special baby who would grow up to be a great king. Mary was very puzzled about this and thought about it a lot.

Some time later Mary and her husband Joseph had to go on a long journey to a town called Bethlehem. They went there because they had to have their names put on a list, rather like a register. When they arrived in Bethlehem there were loads of other people there, also having their names put on the list. All the hotels and guest-houses were full up, but eventually they managed to find somewhere to stay.

Mary was pregnant and while they were staying in Bethlehem her baby was born. They called the baby Jesus. Mary wrapped her lovely baby up and laid him carefully in a box that holds hay for animals to eat.

That same night there were some men looking after their sheep in the fields. All of a sudden a very bright light started to glow in the sky and an angel appeared. The men were really frightened, but the angel told them not to be afraid. The angel had some news for the men. A very special baby had been born who would save people. The angel said that the men should go and visit the baby.

Suddenly the sky was filled with angels singing. The men were absolutely amazed.

When the angels had gone the men were very excited. 'Let's go!' they said. 'Let's go and find this special baby.'

They rushed into the town of Bethlehem and found baby Jesus lying in the hay in the animal feeding box, just as the angel had said. The men told Mary and Joseph all about the bright angels in the sky and their special message. This puzzled Mary all over again.

In a country a long way away some men were studying the stars when they noticed a new star in the sky. They decided to follow the star because it meant that a special king had been born.

Off went the men to King Herod's palace, because they wanted to ask him where the new king was. Now, King Herod was very upset about this news. He didn't want a new king to be born. He was the king. So he told the men to look for the baby, and when they had found where the baby was they should come back and tell him.

So off they went again, following the star. This time they found where Jesus was. They were so pleased. They went to look at baby Jesus and bowed down in front of him. They gave Jesus expensive presents and then they left.

And they did not go back to tell King Herod where the baby was after all, but they went back to their own country.

### Questions to prompt discussion

- Do you think Joe likes to *remember* this story? Why? Why not?
- Which part do you think he might like to *remember* most?
- Where do you think he might hear or read about this story?

▶ ● Using the picture of the child (CD artwork A) or the persona doll, teacher should explain how Joe and other Christians *remember* the story of the birth of Jesus.

▶   Teacher could show an image of Christians in church (see CD artwork 21).

    ○ Joe and other Christians hear the story about the birth of Jesus at Christmas time in a big building called a church.

    ○ Joe has books about the story at home and in school. (Teacher shows a variety of books featuring the nativity story.)

    ○ When Joe is in church at Christmas time they all sing songs about when baby Jesus was born to help them to *remember* the story.

    ○ In the church are little models of Mary, the angels and the men who visited baby Jesus. Joe loves looking at the model of baby Jesus.

    ○ Joe has lots of Christmas cards at home. They have pictures of the story on them. They help Joe *remember* the story.

▶ ● Teacher should duplicate the cards below (or print them from the CD). In pairs or small groups the children sort and select cards that show what helped Joe and other Christians to *remember* the story about the birth of the baby Jesus.

*Figure 3.2*

### *Step 5 Evaluate*

**Is it important for Christians to *remember* the story of the birth of Jesus?**

● Teacher suggests the following scenario for the children to think about.

> One year Joe went on holiday with his mum and dad at Christmas time. They went in a plane to another country called Egypt. They had a lovely time in the sunshine, playing on the beach and swimming in the sea. When they were on holiday, they had no Christmas cards to help them to *remember* the story of baby Jesus, they had no little models to look at, they did not go to church to sing songs about baby Jesus and they did not hear the story about the birth of baby Jesus.
>
> When they got home from their holidays Christmas was all over and Joe had not *remember*ed baby Jesus at all.

**Questions to prompt discussion**

● Do you think it matters that Joe did not *remember* baby Jesus? Why? Why not?

● When he heard that his friends at church had *remembered* the story about baby Jesus, how do you think Joe felt? Why?

● Do you think Joe could have *remembered* the story if he had tried? How would he do that?

● Do you think that hearing the story, seeing the cards and the little models and singing the songs would have helped Joe to *remember*? How?

● Why do you think Joe and other Christians want to *remember* the story about the birth of Jesus?

● The children complete the writing frame below (see Figure 3.3 and CD). The teacher or a classroom assistant scribes if necessary.

Joe likes to remember the story about the birth of baby Jesus because ...

*Figure 3.3*

## Remembering in Buddhism

Children should explore Steps 1, 2 and 3 in the book (pages 45–48) before they engage with Steps 4 and 5 in this section.

### *Step 4 Contextualise*

### How do Buddhists *remember* the Buddha?

- (▶) ● Teacher shows an image (see CD artwork 24a) or a model of the Buddha. The children look very closely and talk about what they notice about it.
- Children paint a picture of the Buddha or make a clay model.
- (▶) ● Teacher could use a picture of a Buddhist child (see CD artwork B) or a Buddhist persona doll (see page 6), called Elsa (or other name), to explore this aspect of the learning. During class discussion teacher explains that Elsa likes to look at the statue of this man, called the Buddha, to help her *remember* him.
- Teacher tells a story about the Buddha (see below).
- Act out the story with the children.

### The Buddha and Devadatta

There was once a wonderful man called the Buddha. He was very kind and thoughtful and was always trying to help people and teach people how to be good and kind to others.

The Buddha had an enemy, though. His enemy was a mean man called Devadatta who was very jealous of the Buddha. Devadatta thought that he was very important and he wanted people to listen to him, not to the Buddha.

One day the Buddha was walking on the slopes of a mountain. Devadatta went to the top of the mountain and hurled a great rock, which went rolling and tumbling dangerously down towards the Buddha. Suddenly, two peaks sprang up from the ground and stopped the rock from rolling any further, and so the Buddha was safe.

Devadatta was furious, but he had another plan. This time he went to the elephant keepers and gave one of the elephants some strong drink to make it get drunk. The poor elephant didn't know what it was doing. It charged around, drunk and angry, crashing into things and doing lots of damage. Everyone was terrified and ran away from the elephant, except the Buddha. He kept on calmly walking towards it.

Suddenly a woman carrying a baby rushed along the street trying to get away from the drunken elephant. As she ran by the Buddha she stumbled and dropped her baby, right in front of the Buddha and right in front of the angry elephant. The elephant was just about to trample on the little baby when the Buddha did something amazing. He calmly put out his hand and stroked the elephant gently on the head. The elephant was instantly calm and peaceful, and bent down on his knees in front of the Buddha. The baby was safe and so was the Buddha.

**Questions to prompt discussion**

- Do you think Elsa and other Buddhists like to *remember* this story? Why?
- Which part of the story do you think Elsa likes to *remember* most? Why?
- What does Elsa *remember* about the Buddha when she hears this story?

- Teacher shows an image of a Buddhist offering flowers at a Buddhist shrine (see CD  artwork 24). Elsa likes to *remember* the Buddha when she takes flowers and puts them in front of the statue.
- Children draw a picture and annotate (the teacher scribes) in the writing/drawing frame provided (see Figure 3.4 and CD).

How do Buddhists remember the Buddha?

*Figure 3.4*

### *Step 5 Evaluate*

### Is it important for Buddhists to *remember* the Buddha?

- Teacher writes the following statements on cards and reads them out to the class, answering the question, 'Why do you think Elsa and other Buddhists want to *remember* the Buddha?'

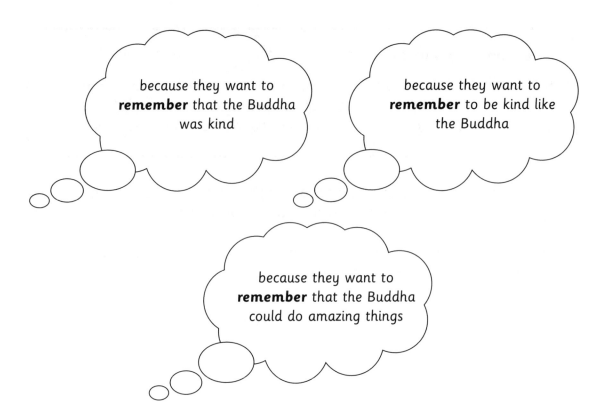

- The children think carefully about which one they agree with.
- When the teacher reads out each statement again, the children raise their hands or stand up if they agree with it.

## Remembering in Hinduism

Children should explore Steps 1, 2 and 3 in the book (pages 45–48) before they engage with Steps 4 and 5 in this section.

### *Step 4 Contextualise*

**How do Hindus *remember* Lord Vishnu at Holi?**
- Teacher shows an image of Lord Vishnu (see CD artwork 25), and asks the children to talk to a partner about what they notice. Discuss as a class.
- Teacher uses a picture of a Hindu child (see CD artwork D) or a Hindu persona doll (see page 6), called Sita (or other name), to explore this aspect of the learning. Explain that Sita likes to *remember* Lord Vishnu. Sita has a special story she loves to hear. Do the children want to hear it too?
- Teacher tells the story below. The children act out the story or draw their favourite part of the story.
- Have a class discussion about the story.

### The story of Lord Vishnu and Prahlad

In a land far, far away lived a boy called Prahlad. He believed in a powerful God called Lord Vishnu and he prayed to Lord Vishnu every day.

Now Prahlad's father was a very mean and wicked man, and he thought that he was so important that people ought to pray to him. 'Pray to me,' he shouted at people. He even shouted, 'Pray to me,' when he saw his son Prahlad.

Prahlad was not happy about this. 'I won't pray to you. You are just an ordinary man. I pray to the God, Lord Vishnu.'

Prahlad's father was absolutely furious. He made some wicked plans. One day he told his servants to dig a deep pit, to put poisonous snakes in it, and then to put Prahlad in the pit with the snakes. When Prahlad was in the pit he prayed to the God, Lord Vishnu, and do you know? Not a single snake went near him.

Another time Prahlad's wicked father made a herd of elephants very angry and excited and they started to charge along towards where Prahlad was. It was very dangerous, but Prahlad remembered Lord Vishnu and prayed to him, and guess what? All the elephants calmed down and stopped before they reached Prahlad. He was saved once more.

Prahlad's father was very mad by this time, so he made a plan with his mean and wicked sister Holika. She had very special magic powers. Her plan was to take Prahlad into a fire. She thought her magic powers would keep her safe. She took Prahlad into the flames of a big bonfire, but guess what? Prahlad remembered Lord Vishnu and prayed to him. Lord Vishnu kept Prahlad perfectly safe and Holika was burned in the fire.

### Questions to prompt discussion

- Do you think Sita likes to *remember* this story? Why? Why not?
- Which part of the story do you think is the most important part to *remember*? Why?
- What do you think Sita and other Hindus *remember* about Lord Vishnu? (Is he old, clever, kind, powerful, ugly?)

- Teacher should show how Sita and other Hindus *remember* Lord Vishnu at a special celebration called Holi:
- Set up a Hindu shrine in the classroom. Show how Sita and other Hindus make offerings at the shrine to Lord Vishnu.
- Look at images of Hindus around a Holi bonfire, burning an effigy of Holika (like a guy at Guy Fawkes' night) (see CD artwork 25a).
- Show an image of Hindus worshipping in a temple at a shrine to Vishnu (see CD artwork 25b).
- Role play the story that helps Hindus to *remember* the God Lord Vishnu.

### *Step 5 Evaluate*

### Is it important for Hindus to *remember* Lord Vishnu?

▶ ● Teacher uses the picture of the child (CD artwork D) or the persona doll to set the scenario below .

> One day Sita was really poorly. She had a bad headache and she had itchy spots all over her tummy. She felt so poorly that she had to spend a few days tucked up in bed. The trouble was, it was a special celebration time. It was the festival of Holi and all her friends were going to the temple to hear the story about Lord Vishnu. They were going to pray at the shrine where there were pictures and models of Lord Vishnu. Poor Sita would not be able to join in.

● Have a class discussion about the situation.

> **Questions to prompt discussion**
>
> ● How do you think Sita feels about missing the Holi celebrations?
> ● Do you think she would be able to *remember* Lord Vishnu if she was not there?
> ● What could she do to try to *remember* Lord Vishnu?
> ● Do you think that she should try to *remember* Lord Vishnu? Why? Why not?

## Remembering in Judaism

Children should explore Steps 1, 2 and 3 in the book (pages 45–48) before they engage with Steps 4 and 5 in this section.

### *Step 4 Contextualise*

### How do Jews *remember* the story about God's help at Passover?

▶ ● Teacher could use a picture of a Jewish child (see CD  artwork C) or a Jewish persona doll (see page 6), called Joshua (or other name), to explore this aspect of the learning. Teacher should tell the children that Joshua loves to *remember* a very special story that his dad tells them every year. Would they like to hear it?
● Teacher tells the story below, told at Passover in Jewish homes.
● Children act out the story, led by the teacher.
● Teacher could organise to role play a Jewish Seder meal with the children, to show how Jewish families *remember* the story. Include the lighting of the candles, sharing the special food on the Seder plate, telling the story and singing a Jewish song.

## God helps the Jews to be free

Many, many years ago in a country a long way away, called Egypt, lived some people called Jews. They were very sad because they were slaves in Egypt. That meant that they had to do loads of really hard work, making roads and building enormous buildings. If they did not work hard enough or fast enough the soldiers in Egypt would hit them. They had no time off and hardly any money. The sad thing was, they were not allowed to leave Egypt. They had to keep on working hard, day after day. It was awful for them.

One day, a man called Moses, who was a Jew, saw a bush on fire. He went closer and heard a great voice coming from the bush. The voice was God speaking. God spoke to Moses and told him that he must go to Egypt and help to get all the Jews out of Egypt so that they would not be slaves any longer. Moses was very worried, but God said that he would help Moses.

So Moses went to Egypt and went to see the king. 'You must let the Jews leave Egypt so that they can be free,' said Moses.

But the king of Egypt would not listen. 'No!' he said.

God helped the Jews by making horrible things happen to the people of Egypt. First of all God made the rivers and lakes turn to blood. Then hundreds and hundreds of frogs came out of the rivers and went into all the houses in Egypt.

'Will you let the Jews leave Egypt now?' asked Moses when he went back to the king of Egypt.

'No!' was the answer again.

So God made more horrible things happen to the people in Egypt. The air was filled with gnats and flies, the animals died, all the people in Egypt got sores all over their bodies, huge hailstones fell from the sky, fat insects ate all the food growing in the fields, and the sky became really dark.

Moses went once more to the king of Egypt. 'Will you let the Jews leave now?' asked Moses.

'No!' answered the king.

But God had another plan. He told the Jews to paint a mark over the doors of their houses, and to be ready to leave Egypt. They all did as God asked, and that night lots of people in Egypt died. But God saved all the Jews, who had marks painted over their doors.

All the people in Egypt were very scared now and wanted the Jews to leave. 'Get out of Egypt!' they shouted. The king of Egypt wanted them to leave too. 'Get out!' he shouted. So all the Jews followed Moses out of Egypt.

God carried on helping the Jews. He showed them the way out of Egypt and through the desert. In the day they followed smoke and in the night they followed flame. They walked a long, long way until they came to a great sea.

'What shall we do?' they all said. 'The people from Egypt will come after us.' But God still looked after the Jews. He made the sea part, making a path for the Jews to cross. Soon they were safe on the other side. God had helped the Jews so that they could be free.

**Questions to prompt discussion**

- Do you think Joshua likes to *remember* this story? Why? Why not?
- Which part of the story do you think he likes to *remember* most? Why?
- What do you think Joshua thinks about God when he *remembers* this story?

### *Step 5 Evaluate*

**Is it important for Jews to *remember* how God helped the people in the story?**

- Teacher should encourage class discussion about the value of *remembering* the story for Jews.

**Questions to prompt discussion**

- Why do you think Joshua and other Jews like to *remember* this story?
- Who do you think is the most powerful person in the story?
- Who do you think the Jews think about most when they *remember* the story? Why do you think that?
- Is it important for Joshua and other Jews to *remember* the story?
- Would it matter if they forgot the story? Why? Why not?
- Do the songs and the special food help Joshua to *remember* the story?
- If they didn't have the special food and sing the songs, would they still *remember* the story or do you think they might forget it?
- Do you think the story helps Joshua to *remember* God? Why? Why not?
- Do you think it is important for Joshua to *remember* God? Why? Why not?

- Use the pictures on the sheet below (also see CD artwork D (1–7)). Children put rings around the things that Jews do to help them to *remember* how God helped the Jews in the story. They can then annotate (teacher or a classroom assistant scribes if necessary).

How do Jews remember the story of how God helped the people leave Egypt?

Jews like to remember this story because ...

*Figure 3.5*

## Remembering in Islam

Children should explore Steps 1, 2 and 3 in the book (pages 45–48) before they engage with Steps 4 and 5 in this section.

### *Step 4 Contextualise*

### How do Muslims *remember* the story about the angel's message for Muhammad (pbuh)?

- The teacher could use a picture of a Muslim child (see CD artwork E) or a Muslim ◀ persona doll (see page 6), called Fatima (or other name), to explore this aspect of the learning. Teacher explains that Fatima has a very special story that she likes to *remember*. Would they like to hear the story? Teacher should tell the story (see below and CD). When the name Muhammad is mentioned, Muslims traditionally say 'Peace ◀ be upon him' (pbuh).
- The teacher continues to use the picture of the child or the persona doll to illustrate how Muslim children *remember* the Qur'an.
  - ○ When Fatima goes to the special Muslim school she learns to *remember* exactly the same words that Muhammad (pbuh) learned when the angel Jibreel spoke to him on the mountain (see CD artwork 25c). ◀
  - ○ She only knows a few words, but when she is older she will *remember* lots more.
  - ○ She learns to *remember* the words in a special language called Arabic. She also learns to write some of the words in Arabic (see CD artwork 7c). ◀
- If there are Muslim children in the class they may be able to share some of the Qur'an in Arabic that they have learned to *remember*. Alternatively, invite a Muslim into school to talk about his or her experience in Muslim school and how he/she learned to *remember* parts of the Qur'an. The visitor should be able to write some Arabic for the children to see. Children could copy and decorate some simple Arabic letters or words for display (see CD artwork 7c). ◀
- Ask the children to *remember* a simple Arabic greeting, 'Salaam alekum', to say to the persona doll or other Muslims.

### An angel visits Muhammad (pbuh)

Many years ago lived a wonderful man called Muhammad (pbuh). He was good and kind and honest and always tried to help people.

Muhammad (pbuh) would always get very upset when he saw people being unkind to others, or if people told lies or stole money. Sometimes he needed to get away from people and think quietly in the mountains and pray to Allah (God).

One day he was up in the mountains where it was quiet and calm, when suddenly a really bright light shone in front of him. He was very scared. The light was so bright that he had to hold his hand in front of his eyes. This light came from the angel Jibreel. Then, Muhammad (pbuh) heard Jibreel's voice. Jibreel told him to speak.

Muhammad (pbuh) was very confused and frightened. 'But I don't know what to say,' he replied. Then, suddenly, he knew what to say. Words tumbled out of his mouth. These were wise and clever words. Jibreel taught Muhammad (pbuh) what to say and Muhammad (pbuh) remembered all of it.

When the angel Jibreel had gone, Muhammad (pbuh) came down the mountain and rushed home. He immediately told his wife all about what had happened. He was still very frightened and confused.

'This is amazing,' said his wife. 'I think this is a special message for you. You should go again and see what happens.'

So Muhammad (pbuh) again went up the mountain, and again the angel Jibreel came to him, and again Muhammad (pbuh) was given special messages. These were special messages from Allah.

Muhammad (pbuh) learned more and more from the angel Jibreel, and then it was time to tell all the people the special messages. He was able to remember all of it.

He started by telling his friends, and then other people began to be interested. More and more people heard Muhammad (pbuh) tell them the messages from Allah. More and more people were able to remember the messages, and more and more people learned about how Allah wanted them to behave.

## Questions to prompt discussion

- Do you think Fatima likes to *remember* this story? Why? Why not?
- Which part of the story do you think she likes to *remember* most? Why?
- What do you think Fatima thinks about Allah when she *remembers* this story?
- What do you think she thinks about Muhammad (pbuh) when she *remembers* the story?

### Step 5 Evaluate

### Is it important for Muslims to *remember* the story of Muhammad (pbuh)?

- Teacher lead class discussion about what the children think about the importance of *remembering* for Muslims.

## Questions to prompt discussion

- Do you think it is important for Fatima to *remember* the story about Muhammad (pbuh) getting the messages from Allah? Why? Why not?
- Do you think it is important for her to *remember* the messages from Allah? Why? Why not?
- Would it matter if she forgot Muhammad (pbuh)?
- Would it matter if she forgot the message?
- What would happen if she forgot Muhammad (pbuh)?
- Do you think that Fatima might want to *remember* everything that Muhammad (pbuh) learned to *remember*? Why? Why not?
- Do you think that it would be easy to *remember* everything that Muhammad (pbuh) learned, or would that be hard?

- Teacher writes on large pieces of paper the following statements:

# because they want their friends to think that they are clever

# because they want to do what Allah wants

# because they love the story about Muhammad (pbuh)

- Teacher asks the question, 'Why do you think Fatima and other Muslims *remember* the story about Muhammad (pbuh) learning to *remember* the message from Allah?'
- Teacher places the statements in different parts of the room and reads out each statement carefully. The children decide which statement they agree with most and stand next to it. (The children may need some encouragement not to go where their friends are going, or where the majority appear to be heading.) There are no right or wrong responses here.

## Remembering in Sikhism

Children should explore Steps 1, 2 and 3 in the book (pages 45–48) before they engage with Steps 4 and 5 in this section.

### *Step 4 Contextualise*

#### How do Sikhs *remember* Guru Nanak?
- Teacher shows a picture of a Sikh parade celebrating Guru Nanak's birthday (see CD ◀ artwork 25e). Teacher asks the children what they notice (for instance: many people, wearing of special clothes, carrying flags, dancing). They are doing this to *remember* a special birthday of someone very important.
- Teachers could use a picture of a Sikh child (see CD artwork F) or a Sikh persona doll ◀ (see page 6), called Amjid (or other name), to explore this aspect of learning. Teacher explains that Amjid enjoys the parade and the celebrations. 'Shall we find out who they want to *remember* during their celebration?'
- Teacher shows a picture of Guru Nanak (see CD artwork 25d). 'Here is the important ◀ person who the Sikh people want to *remember*. He is very special to Amjid, and Amjid likes to *remember* a story about him.'

(▶) ● Tell the story (see below and CD).
● Children can sequence pictures that retell the story of Guru Nanak.
● Children paint and draw pictures that show the ways in which Sikhs *remember* Guru Nanak on his birthday. Put together a class display to show the parade, the flag carrying and the dancing.

## Guru Nanak disappears

Many years ago lived a good man called Nanak. He loved God very much and he spent a lot of time thinking about God and praying to God. Nanak always wanted to feel clean before he prayed to God, so every day he would go to the river and wash himself from head to toe. Then he felt ready to think about God.

One day Nanak went to the river as usual to wash before he prayed, but this time was very different. This time Nanak simply disappeared. He was nowhere to be seen. His clothes were on the riverbank, but there was no sign of Nanak. His friends and family rushed up and down the riverbank shouting for him. 'Nanak, where are you?' they shouted. They were so worried that he may have drowned in the river.

For three days his friends and family searched for Nanak, looking high and low. But then, the next day, they were all amazed. Nanak came back. He was perfectly safe and very calm and quiet.

'Where have you been, Nanak?' they cried. 'We have been so worried about you!'

Nanak quietly explained that he had been talking with God and that God had told him what to do. He told them that God had a special plan for him and that he must tell people all about what God had said to him.

So that is what Nanak did. He travelled around the country teaching people and telling them about God. Crowds of people listened to him wherever he went. They called him Guru Nanak because a guru is a great teacher who can teach people about God. Many people loved Guru Nanak and loved the things he told them.

## Questions to prompt discussion

● Which part of the story do you think Amjid and other Sikhs might like to *remember* most? Why do you think that?
● Do you think the parades and the dancing and the celebrations will help Amjid and other Sikhs to *remember* Guru Nanak? Why? Why not?
● What else could they do to help them to *remember* Guru Nanak?

### *Step 5 Evaluate*

### Is it important for Sikhs to *remember* Guru Nanak?

● Remind the children about the celebrations Sikhs have to help them to *remember* Guru Nanak on his birthday.
● Discuss with the class whether they think it is important for Sikhs to *remember* Guru Nanak.

> **Questions to prompt discussion**
>
> - Do you think Sikhs like to *remember* Guru Nanak? Why? Why not?
> - Do you think it would matter if they forgot about Guru Nanak? Why? Why not?
> - What do they *remember* about Guru Nanak?
> - Which part of the celebrations helps them to *remember* (the picture of Guru Nanak, the dressing in smart clothes, the parade, the flags, the dancing)?
> - Can you think of other things that Sikhs could do to help them to *remember*?

- The children complete the activity sheet provided below (and on CD), with support ◀ from class teacher or support assistant to scribe if necessary.

---

Sikhs like to remember Guru Nanak because ...




This is how Sikhs remember Guru Nanak on his birthday. (Draw a picture.)

---

*Figure 3.6*

## Resources on the CD

### *Figures*

3.1   Writing frame – *someone I remember*

3.1a  Writing frame – *a story I remember*

3.1b  Writing frame – *something that happened that I remember*

3.2   Cards – helping Joe remember the story of the birth of the baby Jesus

3.3   Writing frame – *Joe likes to remember the story of the birth of baby Jesus because*

3.4   Writing frame – *how do Buddhists remember the Buddha?*

3.5   Writing frame – *how do Jews remember the story of how God helped the people leave Egypt*

3.6   Activity sheet – *Sikhs like to remember Guru Nanak because*

### *Artwork*

A.   Joe, a Christian boy
B.   Elsa, a Buddhist girl
C.   Joshua, a Jewish boy
D.   Sita, a Hindu girl
E.   Fatima, a Muslim girl
F.   Amjid, a Sikh boy
7c.   Arabic writing
21.   Joe in church at Christmas
21a–d. Images of the baby Jesus
24.   Elsa offering flowers at a Buddhist shrine
24a.  The Buddha
25.   Lord Vishnu
25a.  A Holi bonfire
25b.  Hindus worshipping at a shrine to Vishnu
D1–7. Helping Jews remember how God helped the people leave Egypt
25c.  Children reading Arabic
25d.  Guru Nanak
25e.  Sikh parade to celebrate Guru Nanak's birthday

## *Stories: Christian*

*The story of the birth of baby Jesus*

## *Stories: Buddhist*

*The Buddha and Devadatta*

## *Stories: Hindu*

*The story of Lord Vishnu and Prahlad*

## *Stories: Jewish*

*God helps the Jews to be free*

## *Stories: Muslim*

*An angel visits Muhammad (pbuh)*

## *Stories: Sikh*

*Guru Nanak disappears*

# Special

The concept *special* has significance within all children's lives, be they from religious or non-religious backgrounds. The idea that certain objects, times, places, people and books are treasured or revered and treated in out-of-the-ordinary ways provides a foundation on which to build later enquiries into *holy* or *sacred* at Key Stage 2. This unit of work explores the concept of *special* exclusively in relation to books in order to focus and clarify the children's learning and avoid overwhelming them with information.

The *special* books explored in this resource have been selected from those religions in which sacred writings play a most obvious, prominent role. (Classes with other faiths represented might wish to explore other *special* books.) The book looks at the Christian *special* book and how is it used. It also provides the following examples from other religions:

What is the Jewish *special* book and how is it used?
What is the Muslim *special* book and how is it used?
What is the Sikh *special* book and how is it used?

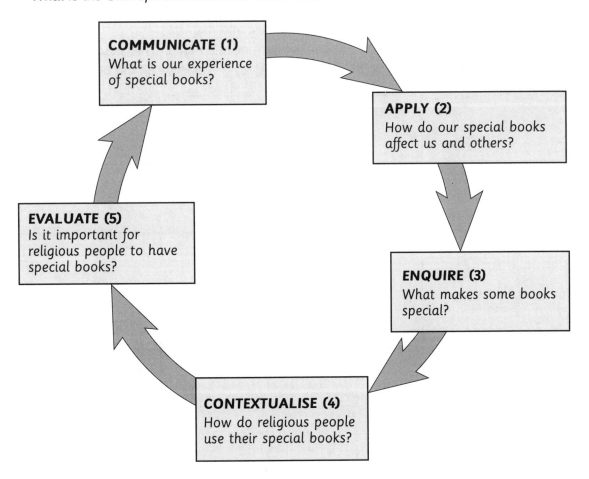

**COMMUNICATE (1)**
What is our experience of special books?

**APPLY (2)**
How do our special books affect us and others?

**ENQUIRE (3)**
What makes some books special?

**CONTEXTUALISE (4)**
How do religious people use their special books?

**EVALUATE (5)**
Is it important for religious people to have special books?

## Special in Christianity

### *Step 1 Communicate*

**What is our experience of *special* books?**

- Ask the children to think about a book that is very *special* to them. They should tell a partner about their *special* book, and share some ideas with the class.
- The children will most readily think of stories that they like. The teacher can now present some alternatives (for instance, 'Here is my *special* book. It is a photograph album which is very *special* because it has pictures of my wedding which I want to remember.' 'Here is my son's first exercise book. My son had it when he was at school. It is a *special* book to him because it reminds him of his first days at school.' 'Here is a book that is very *special* to my friend because it has lots of very useful information which she needs when she goes on holiday.' 'This book is very *special* to my granny because it is very old and it was given to her by her granny, and she loved her very much.').
- Encourages the children to think of other *special* books that they or members of their families have, which are not necessarily favourite story books. Send a note home to parents or carers asking if '*special*' books could be brought into school for a display.
- The teacher should set up the *special* book display in order to illustrate that *special* books are given *special* treatment. Use a clear, safe space, and place some silk or velvet material as a base. Provide a large sign over the display area: 'Our special books', decorated with glitter or sequins perhaps. Note: Those children who have few or no books at home should visit the school library to select a *special* book. All books on the display should be treated with great care and respect.
- Children should complete the labels below (see also CD). This could provide an opportunity for ICT work with the children. Display the labels with the books.

My name is ...

My special book is ...

It is special because ...

*Figure 4.1*

**Questions to prompt discussion**

- What is your *special* book?
- Why is it *special*?
- Will it always be *special* to you? Why? Why not?
- Is it *special* to anyone else?
- Is it *special* for the same reason?

## *Step 2 Apply*

### How do our *special* books affect us and others?

- Teacher should encourage the children to talk about the *special* books in their experience and why they are *special* for different reasons.
- Have class or group discussions about how the children use and treat their *special* books in their homes or in school.
- Make a class *special* book. Include items that are *special* to class members (photographs, poems, pictures, a feather or a *special* button, and so on). Decorate the outside and keep it in a *special* place for the children to look at.

**Questions to prompt discussion**

- Where do you usually keep your *special* book?
- When do you look at it?
- How do you feel when you are looking at it? Why is that?
- Will it always be *special* to you?
- How would you feel if you lost it?
- How would you feel if someone got hold of it and tore it up?
- Do you think you might have other *special* books when you get older?
- Is your book *special* to only you, or is it *special* to other people as well?
- Does anyone have a book that is *special* to lots of people?
- How do all the people feel about that book?
- Can you do anything to an ordinary book to make it *special*?
- What might that be?

## *Step 3 Enquire*

### What makes some books *special*?

- Teacher can duplicate and use the cards below (see Figure 4.2 and CD) with groups of children, or use the statements on the interactive whiteboard to discuss with the whole class. From all the statements, the children should select five that they agree with most. Some children may wish to add more statements to the list.

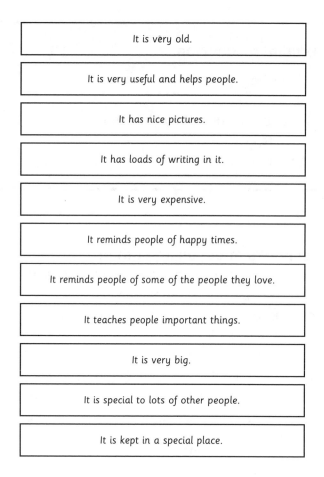

Figure 4.2

### Step 4 Contextualise

**What is the Christian *special* book and how is it used?**
- ● Teacher could use a picture of a Christian child (CD artwork A) or a persona doll (see page 6), called Joe, for example, to explore this aspect of the learning. Also use the image on CD showing a vicar reading from a Bible on a lectern (see CD artwork 3). Teacher can say, 'Joe has a very *special* book. Shall we find out about it?'
  - ○ When Joe goes with his mum to his church he likes to sit at the front so that he can look at the *special* book, the Bible. He knows that the Bible is a very *special* book for all the Christians in the church because it is on the big, shiny, gold eagle. The eagle makes Joe think that if the eagle could fly it would carry the Bible around so that everyone could hear the stories in it (CD artwork 3).
  - ○ The vicar comes up to the eagle and opens the Bible to read a little bit from it. The Bible in church is very big and looks very heavy. Sometimes the words are very long and sometimes Joe doesn't really understand them. Joe knows that the Bible is *special* because everyone stands up when it is read (see CD artwork 3).
  - ○ Joe goes with his friends to a room at the back of the church. When they are in there a Sunday school teacher tells them a story from the Bible. Joe can understand the story when the Sunday school teacher tells it. They all draw pictures about the story.
  - ○ When Joe is at home he sometimes gets his own Bible picture book out. It is very *special* to him so he keeps it in a box to keep it clean. Some of the stories are about how God looks after people and how powerful God is. Sometimes there are stories about Jesus helping people. Joe's mum says that the stories are very, very old indeed.

- Create a display in the classroom of different Bibles for the children to look at.
- Arrange for the children to visit a local church to see the Bible on a lectern. Ask the vicar, priest or minister to explain why the Bible is *special* and how it is used during the church service. Encourage the children to ask questions about the Christian *special* book. The children can take digital pictures of the lectern and the Bible, or draw pictures for display in the classroom.
- Back in the classroom show and remind the children of the statements about what makes a book *special* (see Step 3). Compare this list with the children's findings about the Bible.

### Questions to prompt discussion

- Why do you think the Bible is *special* for Joe and other Christians?
- Does the Bible match up to the important things we thought about *special* books?
- Is there anything extra about the Bible that makes it *special* that we didn't have on our list?
- What do you think Joe and other Christians think is the most *special* thing about the Bible?

### *Step 5 Evaluate*

### Is it important for Christians to have the Bible?
- Teacher tells the story about Joe (see below and CD).

### Joe's special book

Joe had his cousins over on Saturday. It was such fun to have them there for the whole day. They brought their puppy with them too. Joe's mum spent lots of time chatting and laughing with Joe's aunty and Joe and his cousins played with the puppy. They jumped in and out of the paddling pool in the back yard and squirted the water hose at each other. Then they went into Joe's bedroom and made a den under the bed.

By Saturday evening they had all gone home and Joe felt a bit sad. It seemed so quiet after all the fun and laughing. Joe decided that he would get his special book, the Bible picture book, out of its box and look at the pictures. He loved looking at the pictures of Jesus and the fishermen and the people that Jesus made better when they were ill. The pictures helped him remember all the stories that his mum told him. That would cheer him up.

But when Joe looked for it he could not find the Bible or its special box. He looked through his toys, on the window sill and even in his mum's room, but it was nowhere to be found. Mum came to help him look too. Then they looked under the bed. Tucked away in the corner was a mass of chewed-up paper and the box, all covered with teeth marks.

'Oh dear!' said Mum. 'The puppy must have found your book when you were all playing.'

Poor Joe. He was so upset. His most special book was ruined.

**Questions to prompt discussion**

- How do you think Joe felt? Why?
- What would he miss about his *special* book, the Bible?
- Could he look at another book which would cheer him up as much? Why? Why not?
- Do you think all Christians feel like that about their Bibles? Why? Why not?
- If Joe did not have his Bible would he forget about God and Jesus? Why? Why not?

Suddenly, Mum spotted something else under the bed. 'Here it is!' she said. 'The dog was only interested in the box. Your *special* book is safe!'

Joe was so pleased. He sat down straight away and looked at all the pictures, from the beginning to the end.

⏵ ● Children complete the drawing/writing frame below (link on CD).

This is Joe looking at his Bible picture book.

He loves it because ...

*Figure 4.3*

## Special in Judaism

Children should explore Steps 1, 2 and 3 in the book (pages 66–68) before they engage with Steps 4 and 5 in this section.

### Step 4 Contextualise

#### What is the Jewish *special* book and how is it used?

- Teacher could use a picture of a Jewish child (CD artwork C) or a persona doll (see page 6), called Joshua, for example, to explore this aspect of the learning. Also use a picture of the Torah scrolls (see CD artwork 6b). Explain that Joshua loves a very *special* book that is kept somewhere *special*. 'Shall we find out about it?'

  ○ Joshua is quite excited today. It is Simhat Torah day. This is a *special* day for all Jews, when they think about their most *special* book.

  ○ Joshua goes with his family to the big building called a synagogue. There are loads of people coming to the synagogue.

  ○ Joshua really likes it when the *special* cupboard at the front of the synagogue is opened and they can all see what is inside. The cupboard contains the very *special* book, the Torah. Joshua thinks it is funny calling it a book. It is not like a book with pages. It is a very, very long piece of *special* material like thick paper with *special* writing on. It is all rolled up, like a huge kitchen roll, on great big wooden sticks. Joshua knows that it is extremely *special* because it has a beautiful cover on it made of soft material. There are silver ornaments that go over the Torah and over the wooden sticks. Joshua sometimes thinks that the Torah looks like a king with a crown on.

  ○ Today the Torah is taken out of the cupboard and a man rests it on his shoulder. Then he starts to walk around the synagogue. It looks really heavy. Joshua and some of his friends move out of their seats. Today they are remembering how wonderful the Torah is. They skip and hop behind the man carrying the Torah and everyone waves flags and sings. Joshua loves joining in. It is like a parade in the synagogue (see CD artwork 6c).

  ○ Joshua knows that the Torah is very *special*. His dad has told him that it is full of *special* laws and instructions from God It tells them what to eat, what to wear and how they should be kind and helpful to others.

- Invite a Jewish visitor to explain why the Torah is *special* to Jews and how they use it. Visit a synagogue if possible, and encourage the children to ask questions. The children could draw or take digital pictures of the scrolls to display in the classroom. If there are Jewish children in school they may wish to talk about the Torah in their lives.

- Tell the story of Moses on Mount Sinai receiving the commandments (below and on CD).

- Act out the story with the class.

- Display pictures of Torah scrolls in the classroom.

- Make mini Torah scrolls using wooden dowels and strips of paper. Children should try to copy some Hebrew script (see CD artwork 6) on their pieces of paper.

- Show and remind the children of the statements about what makes a book *special* (see Step 3 page 67). Compare this list with the children's findings about the Torah.

## Moses on Mount Sinai

Many, many years ago lived a man called Moses. He was the leader of the Jewish people. God looked after the Jewish people, and God told Moses to lead the Jews into the desert where he would look after them. And there they all were, with their tents and their camels and their goats. They were camped by a great big mountain called Mount Sinai.

Moses went up on to the mountain one day to get away from the crowds, to have some peace and quiet and to talk to God. When Moses was there, God spoke to him.

'Get my people ready,' God said. 'I will come to the mountain where the people will see me.'

So when Moses came down the mountain he told the people what God had said. They all had to get ready for God. They had to wash themselves and their clothes and get ready, for two days.

After two days they all looked up at the mountain and became really scared. It was covered in swirling smoke and clouds, and then the whole mountain started to shake. What was God going to do?

Then there was fire coming out of the mountain. The fire was so hot and powerful. Then they heard a deafening noise like a trumpet, and thunder and lightning flashed across the mountain.

The Jewish people were really scared now. They stayed a long way away from the mountain, shivering and shaking with fear. God was at the top of the mountain, hidden in the fire. Moses spoke to God, and God answered Moses in a voice of thunder.

Then Moses went up the mountain. He was up the mountain for a very long time. It was longer than one day, longer than two days, longer than three days. Moses was up the mountain for forty whole days. The Jewish people were really worried.

Eventually they caught sight of Moses staggering down the mountain. He was quite safe, of course, and he was carrying two great big slabs of stone. On the slabs of stone were special laws and instructions for the Jewish people from God. The laws told them how to behave well, how to love God and how to love each other.

These slabs of stone were so special that they were kept in a very special box, and the Jewish people carried these laws with them everywhere. The Jewish people kept the laws safe for hundreds and hundreds of years.

Now, all those laws from God have been written into each copy of the Torah. Every copy of the Torah has the laws that God gave the Jewish people many, many years ago. That is why the Torah is so very, very special.

## Questions to prompt discussion

- Why do you think the Torah is *special* for Joshua and other Jews?
- Does the Torah match up to the important things we thought about *special* books?
- Is there anything extra about the Torah that makes it *special* that we didn't have on our list?
- What do you think Joshua and other Jews think is the most *special* thing about the Torah?

### Step 5 Evaluate

### Is it important for Jews to have the Torah?

- Teacher tells the story about Joshua (see below).

Joshua and his family were going to the synagogue as usual on Saturday morning. As they walked around the corner they could see a police car outside the synagogue and some policemen and policewomen. Lots of people, who Joshua knew from the synagogue, were standing around looking very worried and upset. Joshua could see that some of the Jewish people were crying. Whatever could have happened?

As they got closer Joshua's dad saw his friend. 'Whatever has happened, my friend?' said Joshua's dad. 'Why is everyone so sad?' The man told them the terrible news. The night before some thieves had broken in to the synagogue, had broken open the special cupboard doors and had taken the copies of the Torah away. How terrible. They felt so upset.

### Questions to prompt discussion

- How do you think Joshua felt? Why?
- What would he miss about his *special* book, the Torah?
- Do you think all Jews feel like that about their Torah? Why? Why not?
- Now Joshua and the Jews do not have the Torah at the synagogue will they forget about the laws God gave to them?
- Will they forget to love God and be kind to people? Why? Why not?

A few minutes later a police car pulled up outside the synagogue. On the back seat were the Torah scrolls. The police had caught the thieves and the Torah scrolls were perfectly safe. Now the Jews' *special* books could be put back in the synagogue.

- Children complete the drawing/writing frame below (see CD Figure 4.4).

This is Joshua looking at the Torah.
It is special for Jews.




He loves it because ...

*Figure 4.4*

## Special in Islam

The children should explore Steps 1, 2 and 3 in the book (pages 66–68) before they engage with Steps 4 and 5 in this section.

### *Step 4 Contextualise*

**What is the Muslim *special* book and how is it used?**

- Teacher could use a picture of a Muslim child (see CD artwork E) or a persona doll (see page 6), called Fatima, for example, to explore this aspect of the learning. Also use the image of the Qur'an (see CD artwork 26). Explain that Fatima has a very *special* book that she loves. 'Shall we find out about it?'
  - Every day after tea Fatima gets her most *special* book, the Qur'an, down from a high shelf, wraps it up and puts it in a *special* bag. Her dad takes her, with her *special* book, in the car to the big building in town called the mosque. There is a classroom she goes to inside the mosque and lots of her friends are there.
  - When Fatima is in the classroom the teacher helps them to practise some *special* writing called Arabic (see CD Arabic script artwork 7c). Then they all learn to read some Arabic words. Fatima needs to learn Arabic so that she can read her *special* book, the Qur'an.

○ During the lesson the teacher asks the children to get out their copies of the Qur'an. Fatima unwraps hers carefully and puts it on a *special* stand (see CD artwork 26a).  All her friends do the same thing. They put the *special* books on stands to show how *special* the Qur'an is to them all.

○ They look at their *special* books and read some of the words. As Fatima practises more and more she will be able to say some parts of the Qur'an off by heart. Some of the older boys and girls can remember long parts of the Qur'an without looking at all. Fatima thinks that they are very clever.

○ Fatima's dad has told her that the Qur'an is a very old and very *special* book because everything in it came from Allah (God). It tells Muslims how they should always be kind, good and honest with other people.

○ Fatima works very hard to learn the Qur'an because she feels as if that is what Allah (God) wants her to do. It makes her very happy when she can read new words in her *special* book.

○ When Fatima is at home her mum reads some parts of the Qur'an to her. She loves to hear the words and it teaches her how to be a good person.

● Teacher may wish to make reference to the story of the revelation of the Qur'an to Muhammad (pbuh) in the unit of work on *Remembering*, Step 4 (see CD An angel  visits Mohammad (phuh)).

● Invite a Muslim visitor to explain why the Qur'an is *special* to Muslims and how they use it. Encourage the children to ask questions. If there are Muslim children in school they may wish to talk about the Qur'an in their lives.

● Display a Qur'an on its stand in the classroom. (Teachers should wash their hands before handling the Qur'an.) Ensure that it is in a high position above all other books and that it is not handled by the children in class.

● Show and remind children of the statements about what makes a book *special* (see Step 3 page 67). Compare this list with the children's findings about the Qur'an.

---

**Questions to prompt discussion**

● Why do you think the Qur'an is *special* for Fatima and other Muslims?
● Does the Qur'an match up to the important things we thought about *special* books?
● Is there anything extra about the Qur'an that makes it *special* that we didn't have on our list?
● What do you think Fatima and other Muslims think is the most *special* thing about the Qur'an?

---

### Step 5 Evaluate

### Is it important for Muslims to have the Qur'an?

● Teacher tells the story about Fatima (see below and CD).

Fatima went to the mosque as usual on Thursday evening. After her Arabic lessons she was going to her friend's house to play in her garden. She did not want to take her special book, the Qur'an, with her in case she left it at her friend's house by mistake. Her teacher at the mosque said that it would be safe if she left it in the classroom in the mosque. Fatima could collect it the next day.

Fatima and her friend had a lovely time. The next day Fatima and her family got ready to go to the mosque. Fatima was looking forward to collecting her Qur'an from the mosque classroom. As Fatima's dad parked the car near the mosque they could hear a fire engine and could see lots of smoke over the rooftops.

They rushed around the corner and were very shocked. There was smoke coming out of some of the windows of the mosque and firefighters were trying to put out the blaze. This was terrible!

'It is not so bad,' they heard someone say. 'Everyone is safe. There are no people in the mosque. The fire was very small and was in the classroom. Everything in the classroom is burnt, but the rest of the mosque is not damaged at all.'

Fatima was really upset. Her very special book, the Qur'an, was in the classroom and had been destroyed.

### Questions to prompt discussion

- How do you think Fatima felt? Why?
- What would she miss about her *special* book, the Qur'an?
- Could she read another book which would make her feel as if she was doing what Allah wanted her to do? Why? Why not?
- Do you think all Muslims feel like that about their Qur'an? Why? Why not?
- If Fatima did not have her Qur'an would she forget about Allah?
- Would she forget to be kind to people? Why? Why not?

Then Fatima could see her teacher from the mosque. She was rushing towards them. 'It is OK. I have your Qur'an!' she called. Fatima was so relieved. The teacher had decided to put Fatima's Qur'an in a *special* locked cupboard in the mosque. It had been perfectly safe all the time.

▶ • The children complete the drawing/writing frame below (also on CD). Some Muslim children may not wish to draw the human form and should only draw the Qur'an if they prefer.

This is Fatima reading her Qur'an.
It is a special book for Muslims.

She loves it because ...

*Figure 4.5*

## Special in Sikhism

The children should explore Steps 1, 2 and 3 in the book (pages 66–68) before they engage with Steps 4 and 5 in this section.

### *Step 4 Contextualise*

### What is the Sikh *special* book and how is it used?

- The teacher could use a picture of a Sikh child (see CD artwork F) or a persona doll  (see page 6), called Amjid, for example, to explore this aspect of the learning. Also use a picture of the Guru Granth Sahib (see CD artwork 8b). Explain that Amjid loves a very *special* book that is kept somewhere *special*. 'Shall we find out about it?'
  - Amjid goes to the big building called the gurdwara every week with his family. He knows that the most important thing in the whole building is the *special* book called the Guru Granth Sahib. When Amjid goes into the big main room he can see the *special* book on a platform right at the front. It rests on some cushions and a beautiful gold cloth. There are flowers around the throne where the *special* book is sitting.
  - Amjid loves to look at the person who is sitting behind the *special* book. He has a fan in his hand and he waves this over the *special* book, just as if it were a person that he is keeping cool. He also reads from the book to all the people there (see CD artwork 26b).
  - Soon the music and drums start to play. They all listen to the singing and the music. The words are from the Guru Granth Sahib, the *special* book. They are very

old. They are all about how wonderful God is. They remind Amjid and other Sikhs about how they should help other people.

○ A few weeks ago Amjid's granddad had been chosen to carry the *special* book, the Guru Granth Sahib, to its *special* platform in the main room. This was such an important thing to do. Amjid could see into the *special* room where the Guru Granth Sahib was kept. It was in a bed, just as if it was a person. The *special* book was wrapped up in beautiful cloth and placed on a cushion. Amjid's granddad carried it very gently and carefully over his head. Everyone bowed down as the book, the Guru Granth Sahib, went past. In the evening Amjid's granddad had to carry the Guru Granth Sahib back again to its *special* bed.

○ Amjid's granddad told him that they all look after the Guru Granth Sahib as if it were a very important person. It reminds them that it is like a great teacher for all the Sikh people.

● Invite a Sikh visitor to explain why the Guru Granth Sahib is *special* to Sikhs and how they use it. Visit a gurdwara if possible, and encourage the children to ask questions. If there are Sikh children in school they may wish to talk about the Guru Granth Sahib in their lives.

● Display pictures of Guru Granth Sahib in the classroom.

● Show and remind the children of the statements about what makes a book *special* (see Step 3 page 65). Compare this list with the children's findings about the Guru Granth Sahib.

---

### Questions to prompt discussion

● Why do you think the Guru Granth Sahib is *special* for Amjid and other Sikhs?

● Does the Guru Granth Sahib match up to the important things we thought about *special* books?

● Is there anything extra about the Guru Granth Sahib that makes it *special* that we didn't have on our list?

● What do you think Amjid and other Sikhs think is the most *special* thing about the Guru Granth Sahib?

---

### *Step 5 Evaluate*

### Is it important for Sikhs to have the Guru Granth Sahib?

▶ ● Teacher tells the story about Amjid (see below and CD).

### Amjid's special book

Amjid and his family were on their way to the big meeting place, the gurdwara, when a fire engine went rushing by with its sirens screaming. It was very frightening. Amjid wondered where the fire might be.

When they walked around the corner they could see straight away. The fire was at the gurdwara. There was a big crowd watching the firefighters put out the flames. Amjid's auntie came up to them. She looked really upset.

'Is everyone all right?' asked Amjid's mum.

'Yes, everyone is safe,' said Amjid's aunty. 'It was only a small fire, but something terrible has happened. The fire was in the room where the Guru Granth Sahib is kept. What an awful thing to happen.'

**Questions to prompt discussion**

- How do you think Amjid felt? Why?
- What would he miss about his *special* book, the Guru Granth Sahib?
- Do you think all Sikhs feel like that about their Guru Granth Sahib? Why? Why not?
- Now Amjid and the Sikhs do not have the Guru Granth Sahib at the gurdwara will they forget about God and how to be good to other people? Why? Why not?

A few minutes later Amjid noticed some firefighters coming out of the building. They were carrying something very carefully all wrapped up in a blanket. 'The book is safe!' they shouted. 'It has not been damaged by the fire at all.' A loud cheer went up from all the people that were there. Their *special* book had been saved.

- Children complete the drawing/writing frame below (see CD).

This is Amjid looking at the Guru Granth Sahib.
It is special for Sikhs.

He loves it because ...

*Figure 4.6*

## Resources on the CD

### *Figures*

4.1   Labels – *special books*
4.2   Cards – *what makes books special*
4.3   Writing frame – *Joe looking at his Bible*
4.4   Writing frame – *Joshua looking at the Torah*
4.5   Writing frame – *Fatima reading her Qur'an*
4.6   Writing frame – *Amjid looking at the Guru Granth Sahib*

### *Artwork*

A.     Joe, a Christian boy
C.     Joshua, a Jewish boy
E.     Fatima, a Muslim girl
F.     Amjid, a Sikh boy
3.     Vicar reading from a Bible on a lectern
6.     Hebrew script
6b.    Torah scrolls
6c.    Simhat Torah celebrations
7c.    Arabic script
8b.    The Guru Granth Sahib
26.    The Qur'an
26a.   Fatima reading the Qur'an
26b.   The people listen to the Guru Granth Sahib

### *Stories: Christian*

*Joe's special book*

### *Stories: Jewish*

*Moses on Mount Sinai*
*Joshua's special book*

### *Stories: Muslim*

*Fatima's special book*

### *Stories: Sikh*

*Amjid's special book*

# Authority

The term *authority* is not one young children would normally use. They have a clear understanding, however, that some people can be 'the boss' or 'in charge' and can tell others what to do. Enquiring into this concept with young children should enable them to engage with some ways people express their *authority,* and help them recognise that people have *authority* for a variety of reasons. This concept or key idea will form a foundation for exploring the concepts of *leadership* and *prophethood* when they are older. For religious education the concept of *authority* is of fundamental importance. Key religious figures have demonstrated their *authority,* and it is this that makes them stand out above others. In this book the *authority* of Jesus is explored within Christianity. It also provides the following examples from other religions:

How did the Buddha show his *authority*?
How did Mohammed (pbuh) show his *authority*?
How did Guru Nanak show his *authority*?

In this unit the children start at the **enquire** element of learning so that they can investigate the meaning of the concept before exploring it within the religions and before reflecting on their own experiences of *authority*.

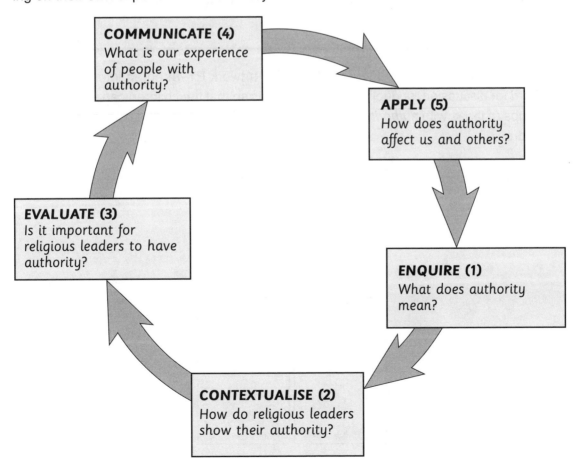

**COMMUNICATE (4)**
What is our experience of people with authority?

**APPLY (5)**
How does authority affect us and others?

**EVALUATE (3)**
Is it important for religious leaders to have authority?

**ENQUIRE (1)**
What does authority mean?

**CONTEXTUALISE (2)**
How do religious leaders show their authority?

## Authority in Christianity

### *Step 1 Enquire*

### What does *authority* mean?

- Teacher should discuss with the children who they think tells them what to do, and through this discussion introduce the term *authority*.

> #### Questions to prompt discussion
>
> - Who has *authority* at home? Who tells you what to do and what not to do?
> - Do you have *authority* over anyone at home (e.g. your little brother, the dog, the guinea pig)?
> - How do you show that you have *authority*?
> - Do some people at home have more *authority* than others? Why is that?

- Discuss with the children who they think has *authority* in school, and extend the discussion to people with *authority* outside school.

> #### Questions to prompt discussion
>
> - Who has *authority* over you at school?
> - How do the teachers show their *authority*?
> - Who has *authority* over the teachers at school, do you think?
> - Which people have *authority* outside school? Who can tell other people what to do?

- Use the cards below (see Figure 5.1 and CD artwork E1–8) on an interactive whiteboard for discussion, or duplicate them into sets so that the children can sort them into groups of those with *authority* and those without. Then pursue the discussion with the children.

*Figure 5.1*

**Questions to prompt discussion**

- Do you think that these people have *authority* all the time? Why? Why not?
- A doctor has *authority* in a hospital but when the doctor goes out and a police-woman tells the doctor not to park in a certain place, who has the greatest *authority* then? Why?
- Can people have *authority* in some places and not in others?
- Why do people have *authority*, do you think?

- Put the list below (see Figure 5.2 and CD) on the whiteboard or duplicate it onto  paper. Discuss the statements with the children. Ask the children to vote for two or three statements that they think are most important. Which statements get the most votes?

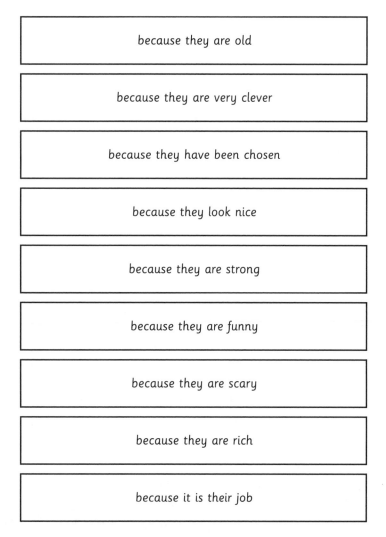

| because they are old |
| because they are very clever |
| because they have been chosen |
| because they look nice |
| because they are strong |
| because they are funny |
| because they are scary |
| because they are rich |
| because it is their job |

*Figure 5.2 Why do some people have authority*

- The children complete the writing/drawing frame below (see Figure 5.3 and CD).

*Figure 5.3*

### *Step 2 Contextualise*

### How did Jesus show his *authority*?

 ● Teacher could use a picture of a Christian child (see CD artwork A) or a Christian persona doll (see page 6), called Joe (or other name), to explore this aspect of the learning. The teacher can say, 'Joe has some stories about someone with *authority*. Shall we find out about him?'

　　○ When Joe goes to church with his mum he hears lots of stories about Jesus. The stories are in the Bible, the special book for Christians. Lots of the stories are about Jesus having *authority*. Jesus could tell people what to do, and sometimes he even told the weather what to do.

　　○ Joe thinks that Jesus was very clever, very kind and very powerful. He thinks that it is still very important to do what Jesus said about being kind to people.

　　○ Joe's mum says that Jesus has more *authority* over them and other Christians than anyone else in the whole world. For them he is the most important boss there could be.

　　○ When Joe goes to Sunday school in the church, the Sunday school teacher tells the children stories about Jesus' *authority*.

● Teacher should tell the three stories below (also see CD) about Jesus showing *authority*. Telling the stories on consecutive days would be effective, with time allowed for reinforcement activities.

● After each story discuss some key points with the class.

**Questions to prompt discussion**

- Do you think that Joe and other Christians like this story? Why? Why not?
- Which part of the story do you think Joe likes best?
- Which part of the story shows that Jesus has *authority* do you think?
- Why did Jesus have *authority*, do you think? Show and remind the children of the list in Step 1 (page 83) about why some people have *authority* ('because they are old, because they are clever', and so on).

- Children can act out each story.
- Use the stories for literacy work.
- Children create a frieze or sequence pictures to illustrate each story.
- Children can complete the drawing/writing frame (see CD Figure 5.4).

### Jesus shows his authority in the temple

Many, many years ago lived a young boy called Jesus. He lived with his mother and his father. When Jesus was 12 years old, they all went on a long journey to a town quite a long way away for a special celebration.

After the celebration they set off for home again, with a large group of people. Jesus' mother and father thought that Jesus was in the group with them, but when they looked he was not there. They started to get quite worried.

Straight away they went back to the town that they had left and they hunted high and low for Jesus. Eventually they found him. He was in a great big important building called a temple. This was where everyone went to pray and to think about God. This was where all the important men in the town went to talk about God and to study their special books about God.

There sat Jesus, with all these important men. They were asking Jesus questions about their special books and about God, and Jesus was so clever that he could tell the important men all the answers. Everyone was amazed that Jesus had such authority, and he was only 12 years old.

### Jesus has authority over the fishermen

A long, long time ago lived a man called Jesus. Jesus was very good and kind and he wanted to tell people all about God and about how to live good lives.

One day he was walking by the seashore and he saw two men fishing from their boat. Jesus called out to the men. 'Come with me,' he called, 'and I will teach you how to catch men.'

At once the two fishermen stopped what they were doing. They came ashore and went with Jesus. Jesus had authority over these men, and they did what he said straight away.

### Jesus has authority over the storm

Many hundreds of years ago lived a man called Jesus. One day he was in a boat with his friends. He was very tired and he fell asleep.

After a little while a strong wind picked up and a terrible storm came. There were big waves crashing against the boat and the wind whistled around them. Jesus' friends were very scared. They thought that the boat might go under the waves. 'Wake up! Wake up!' they shouted to Jesus. 'We might die!' they yelled.

Jesus woke up. 'Why are you so frightened?' he said. With that, Jesus stood up in the boat and told the wind and the waves to stop. Straight away, the wind stopped and the waves calmed down and all was still. Jesus had authority to tell even the storm to stop, and it did. All Jesus' friends were absolutely amazed (see  CD artwork 27).

This is a story that Christians tell. It shows them that Jesus had authority.

Picture

*Figure 5.4*

### *Step 3 Evaluate*

### Is it important for Christians that Jesus has *authority*?

● Teacher should ask the children to imagine what it would be like if each of the stories had a different ending.

**Questions to prompt discussion**

- What if Jesus went into the temple with all the clever men and he didn't know anything about their special books? What if Jesus didn't know the answers to the questions they asked him? Would they have thought he had any *authority* then?
- What if Jesus had called to the men fishing in their boat and they had shouted back, 'No, we are not coming with you. We are too busy fishing!' Would the story have shown that Jesus had *authority* if it had that as an ending?
- What if Jesus had got up in the boat and told the wind and the waves to stop and nothing had happened? What if the storm had carried on? Would that be a story that showed Jesus had *authority*?
- Would Joe and other Christians like to hear those stories if they did not show that Jesus had *authority*? Why? Why not?
- What would Joe and other Christians think about Jesus if he had not shown *authority*?
- Why do you think that Joe and other Christians like to hear those stories about Jesus showing his *authority*?

- The teacher duplicates the cards provided (see Figure 5.5 and CD). The children sort them into groups of statements that they agree or disagree with, or perhaps select three or four cards that they agree with most. The children work in pairs or threes. There are no correct or incorrect responses here, but the children should be encouraged to discuss the statements and why they agree or disagree with them.

| because the stories have a happy ending |
| --- |

| because he likes the pictures that go with the stories |
| --- |

| because they remind him that Jesus can help people |
| --- |

| because they show that Jesus could do amazing things that other people could not do |
| --- |

| because his mum likes the stories too |
| --- |

| because they show that Jesus was very clever |
| --- |

| because he likes the way the Sunday school teacher tells the stories |
| --- |

| because they remind him that Jesus is very important to Christians |
| --- |

*Figure 5.5 Why does Joe like the stories about Jesus showing his authority?*

### *Step 4 Communicate*

### What is our experience of people with *authority*?

- Teacher directs the children to think of an experience when someone has shown their *authority* (for instance, when a teacher, Mum or Dad, a policeman or policewoman, or a nurse has told them or someone else what to do). The children tell a partner and share a few ideas with the class.
- Act out some simple scenarios that show someone with *authority*.
- Teacher should ask the children why the person has *authority* in each scenario, with reference to the statements in Step 1 (page 83: 'because they are old, because they are clever,' and so on).
- Teacher directs the children to consider a time when they have had *authority*. They should tell a partner and share ideas with the class.

### Questions to prompt discussion

- When have you had *authority*?
- How did you feel about that?
- Do you have any *authority* at home?
- Do you wish that you had more *authority* at home? Why? Why not?
- Do you wish you could have *authority* in other places?
- Do you think you will have *authority* when you are older?
- Do you always like it when people show their *authority*? Why? Why not?
- Are there some times when you wish that people did not have *authority*? When is that?

### *Step 5 Apply*

### How does *authority* affect us and others?

- Teacher asks the children to think of situations when *authority* has a good effect, such as when some the children are being unkind in the playground and a dinner lady tells them to stop, or when a doctor tells a patient to take some medicine, or when a fire-fighter tells people to move away from a burning building because it is not safe. The children will have their own experiences of good *authority* and how it affected them. Share ideas in the class.
- Teacher asks the children to think of occasions when *authority* has a bad effect, such as when an older boy or girl says he or she will hurt you if you don't give up your chocolate, or when an adult stranger says they will take you home in their car (Stranger Danger!), or when a thief goes into a shop and says, 'Give me all the cash!' The children will have their own experiences of bad *authority* and how it affected them. Share ideas in the class.
- The children can choose to draw or paint a picture of situations of bad or good *authority* and annotate it. Display the results.

## Authority in Buddhism

Children should explore Step 1 in the book (pages 82–84) before they engage with Steps 2 and 3 in this section. This should then be followed by Steps 4 and 5 in the book (page 88).

### *Step 2 Contextualise*

#### How did the Buddha show his *authority*?

- Teacher could use a picture of a Buddhist child (see CD artwork B) or a Buddhist  persona doll (see page 6), called Elsa (or another name), to explore this aspect of the learning. Teacher can say, 'Elsa has some stories about someone with *authority*. Shall we find out about him?'
  - ○ Elsa loves to hear stories about the Buddha. He lived a long time ago, but there are lots of amazing stories about him.
  - ○ When Elsa goes to the temple with her friends, the monks (the men who live at the temple and teach people about the Buddha) sometimes tell them stories about the Buddha. The monks say that the Buddha was so clever that he had loads of *authority*. Many people went to him to learn about what to do and how to live.
  - ○ The monks say that the Buddha was such a great and good teacher that all the things he taught still have *authority* for them today. They say that he is the most important teacher that there could ever be.
- Teacher should tell the stories below (also see CD) about the Buddha showing *author-*  *ity*. Telling the stories on consecutive days would be effective, with time allowed for reinforcement activities.
- After each story discuss some key points with the class.

> ### Questions to prompt discussion
>
> - Do you think that Elsa and other Buddhists like this story? Why? Why not?
> - Which part of the story do you think Elsa likes best?
> - Which part of the story shows that the Buddha has *authority* do you think?
> - Why did the Buddha have *authority*, do you think? Show and remind the children of the list in Step 1 (page 88) about why some people have *authority* ('because they are old, because they are clever', and so on).

- Children can act out each story.
- Use the stories for literacy work.
- Children create a frieze or sequence pictures to illustrate each story.
- Children complete the drawing/writing frame provided (see CD Figure 5.6).

Note: Buddhism is enormously diverse. Some Buddhist traditions tell different versions and interpretations of the stories. The stories have more significance within the beliefs and practices of some traditions than in others.

## The Buddha and Mara

The Buddha lived a long, long time ago. He was a very good and kind man, and he wanted to find out why there was suffering in the world and how people might be able to stop their suffering. He thought and he thought, and he tried to concentrate his mind. He sat calmly and quietly, day after day, until he felt as if he was getting very close to the answer.

Mara was mean and wicked. He did not want the Buddha to understand all about life and how to overcome suffering, so Mara set about to try to stop him.

The Buddha was sitting under a tree, deep in calm thoughts. Mara got his armies together to attack the Buddha. The wicked armies attacked from all sides, from the front, from the back and all around the Buddha. Mara himself joined in the attack, riding on an elephant.

But the Buddha had authority. He called on ten wonderful beings to defend him. The wonderful beings were so powerful that Mara's armies all ran away.

That was not the end of the story, however. Mara still wanted the Buddha to stop his calm concentration. He still wanted to prevent the Buddha from finding the answer to how to release people from suffering. So Mara set out to cause an argument.

Mara said that the seat where the Buddha sat was his seat. All Mara's wicked followers started to shout in agreement. They all said that the seat where the Buddha sat belonged to Mara. There was no one else there to stand up for the Buddha.

The Buddha was very calm and quiet. He touched the ground with his finger and asked the earth to speak up for him. And the earth did. The earth roared back that the Buddha was telling the truth. The Buddha had authority even over the earth. Mara and his wicked followers had to run away in shame.

## The Buddha and the messengers

The Buddha's father was a great king who lived in a palace. The Buddha had left the palace years before. He had left all his riches and had decided to live a simple life and to teach people how to live. He wanted to teach people that if they lived a certain way, they would learn how to stop suffering.

The Buddha's father, the king, was a good, kind man. He missed his son and wanted to see him. So the king sent messengers to tell the Buddha that he was invited to the palace to visit his father.

The Buddha was a great teacher and he had a lot of authority. Each messenger that was sent saw that the Buddha led a simple life and that the people around him were so happy living that life. So every time a messenger arrived from the king with a message for the Buddha, the messenger stayed.

**The Buddha's wisdom (see CD artwork 28)**

When the Buddha was young he was a Prince and he lived in a palace with his father, the King. The King loved the Prince dearly and wanted the very best for his wonderful son, so he sent for the very best teachers in the country to teach him.

After just a few days the teachers came to the King. 'We cannot teach your son any more,' they said. 'We have only had a few lessons with him and he has learned everything we can teach him. He has such *authority* that he has even been able to teach us things that we did not know.'

The Prince's father was so proud of him. Many years later the Prince became a great teacher called the Buddha.

Figure 5.6

## *Step 3 Evaluate*

### Is it important for Buddhists that the Buddha has *authority*?

● Teacher should ask the children to imagine what it would be like if each of the stories had a different ending.

**Questions to prompt discussion**

- What if the wicked Mara had defeated the Buddha when he and his armies attacked? What would Elsa and other Buddhists think about the Buddha if that had happened in the story?
- What if the Buddha had asked the earth to speak up for him and there had been silence? Would Elsa still think the story is important?
- If all the King's messengers had come back from seeing the Buddha, and had not been changed at all, would the story show the Buddha's *authority*?
- What if the Buddha had not been able to learn anything from the very best teachers? What if the Buddha had not taught the teachers anything? Would they have thought he had any *authority* then?
- Would Elsa and other Buddhists like to hear those stories if they did not show that the Buddha had *authority*? Why? Why not?
- What would Elsa and other Buddhists think about the Buddha if he had not shown *authority* do you think?
- Why do you think that Elsa and other Buddhists like to hear those stories about the Buddha showing his *authority*?

- Teacher should duplicate the cards provided below. The children sort them into groups of statements that they agree or disagree with, or perhaps select three or four statements that they agree with most. The children work in pairs or threes. There are no correct or incorrect responses here, but the children should be encouraged to discuss the statements and why they agree or disagree with them.

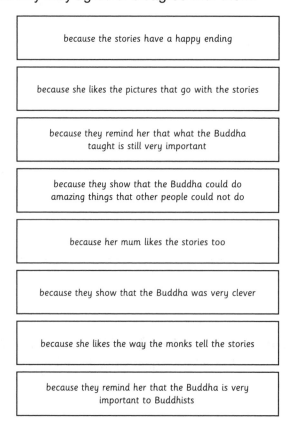

because the stories have a happy ending

because she likes the pictures that go with the stories

because they remind her that what the Buddha taught is still very important

because they show that the Buddha could do amazing things that other people could not do

because her mum likes the stories too

because they show that the Buddha was very clever

because she likes the way the monks tell the stories

because they remind her that the Buddha is very important to Buddhists

*Figure 5.6a Why does Elsa like the stories about the Buddha showing authority?*

Return to the book (page 88) to Steps 4 and 5, to complete the cycle of learning.

## Authority in Islam

The children should explore Step 1 in the book (pages 82–84) before they engage with Steps 2 and 3 in this section. This should then be followed by Steps 4 and 5 in the book (page 88).

### *Step 2 Contextualise*

### How did Muhammad (pbuh) show his *authority*?

- Teacher could use a picture of a Muslim child (see CD artwork E) or a Muslim persona doll (see page 6), called Fatima (or other name), to explore this aspect of the learning. Teacher can say, 'Fatima has some stories about someone with *authority*. Shall we find out about him?'
  - When Fatima and her friends go to the classroom at the mosque she learns stories about Muhammad (pbuh). Her Muslim teachers say that Muhammad (pbuh) was a perfect human being.
  - Fatima loves hearing stories about Mohammad (pbuh). He was very kind and good to people. He was always very fair. The stories remind Fatima that Muhammad (pbuh) was given *authority* by Allah (God) to show other people how to live good lives.
  - Fatima's dad has told her that Allah (God) has *authority* in the world and in the entire universe. Muhammad (pbuh) is Allah's special messenger.
- Teacher should tell the stories below (and on CD) about Muhammad (pbuh) showing *authority*. Telling the stories on consecutive days would be effective, with time allowed for discussion or writing activities.
- After each story discuss some key points with the class.

---

**Questions to prompt discussion**

- Do you think Fatima and other Muslims like this story? Why? Why not?
- Which part of the story do you think Fatima likes best?
- Which part of the story shows that Muhammad (pbuh) has *authority,* do you think?
- Why did Muhammad (pbuh) have *authority*, do you think? Show and remind the children of the list in Step 1 (page 83) about why some people have *authority* ('because they are old, because they are clever', and so on).

---

- Use the stories for literacy work.
- The children can complete the writing frame below (see Figure 5.7 and CD).

Note: There are no images of Muhammad (pbuh) within Islam, and it would be inappropriate for Muslim children to act out the stories or produce any pictures of Muhammad (pbuh) or any human form.

## The fire at the Kabah (see CD artwork 29)

The Kabah is a huge stone building in the shape of a cube. It is very, very old and has been used for hundreds of years as a place to worship Allah (God).

One day, a long time ago, there was a terrible fire at the Kabah and it was very badly damaged. What had been saved, however, was the very special, shiny, black stone that had been laid in the corner of the Kabah hundreds of years before.

There were many different tribes living near the Kabah at the time. All these different groups of people worked very hard to build the Kabah again.

At last it was finished and the time came to place the very important black stone in the wall of the Kabah. The trouble was that every tribe wanted to do this special task. They all started to argue about who should lay the stone. At last they agreed that the next person to walk into the courtyard would be the person to settle the argument.

Muhammad (pbuh) was the next person to walk into the courtyard. Muhammad (pbuh) was a very good and kind man and he always made good decisions.

The people told him about the problem. Muhammad (pbuh) spread out a large sheet on the ground and placed the special black stone in the centre. He then told the leaders of each tribe to lift the edges of the sheet and carry the stone together to the Kabah.

The people could see that Muhammad (pbuh) had authority. They did as he told them and Muhammad (pbuh) himself lifted the black stone to be placed in the wall. Everyone was happy.

## Muhammad (pbuh) spreads the message

Muhammad (pbuh) lived many, many years ago in a town called Makah. He had received messages from Allah (God). Allah had given Muhammad (pbuh) the authority to tell others about how to live good lives. Allah had said that people should be fair, that they should be thoughtful and that they should be kind.

Muhammad (pbuh) was busy telling people in Makah about what Allah had told him. More and more people listened to him and decided to change their lives and do as he said. People could see that Muhammad (pbuh) had authority and they wanted to live in a way that would please Allah.

## Muhammad (pbuh) leads an army

Muhammad (pbuh) lived a long time ago in a town called Makah. Allah (God) had given Muhammad (pbuh) authority to tell others how to behave and how to live good lives. Muhammad (pbuh) spent his time teaching people about what Allah had told him. Muhammad (pbuh) was Allah's special messenger. Many people loved listening to the message Muhammad (pbuh) was telling them, and more and more people followed him to hear what he had to say.

But there were some enemies about. Some people could see how the crowds listened to Muhammad (pbuh) and his message from Allah, and they were jealous. They were worried that he might get too powerful, so they planned to harm him.

Muhammad (pbuh) realised that he was in danger. He and his friends and followers had to run away from Makah. They went to another town called Madinah, and made their home there. Muhammad (pbuh) had authority from Allah and made rules for the people in Madinah so that they could live good lives.

Back in Makah the enemies of Muhammad (pbuh) were still planning to do harm. They were even more worried about all the hundreds of people who were listening to Muhammad (pbuh) and his message from Allah. So they thought that they would be very clever and give out weapons to all the enemies of Muhammad (pbuh).

Muhammad (pbuh) heard about this. He realised that he would have to return to Makah to try to get all the people there to listen to the message from Allah and to change their lives. But how could he do that? He did not want to have a huge fight where people would get hurt.

What he did was call an army together. His plan was to frighten the people of Makah and make them surrender and let him back into the town without any fighting.

Muhammad (pbuh) had authority over his army. When they reached the outside of Makah he told them to spread out. When it got dark that night he told each man to light a small fire. They did as Muhammad (pbuh) had told them, and when the people of Makah saw all the fires, they were terrified. They thought that around each fire would be a large camp of soldiers.

So they gave up immediately. They let Muhammad (pbuh) and his army back into Makah and there had been no fighting at all.

This is a story that is important to Muslims.
It shows that Muhammad (pbuh) had authority.

*Figure 5.7*

### Step 3 Evaluate

### Is it important for Muslims that Muhammad (pbuh) had *authority*?

- Teacher should discuss with the children some of the following points.
  - ○ Do you think Fatima and other Muslims like these stories?
  - ○ Why do you think that they are important?
  - ○ Which story do you think is the best one for showing the *authority* of Muhammad (pbuh)? Why do you think that?
  - ○ Who gave Muhammad (pbuh) *authority* to tell others what to do?
  - ○ Do you think it is important that Allah (God) gave Muhammad (pbuh) his *authority*? Why? Why not?
- Teacher should duplicate the cards provided below (also see CD Figure 5.8). The children sort them into groups of statements that they agree or disagree with, or perhaps select three or four that they think are the most important. The children work in pairs or threes. There are no correct or incorrect responses here, but the children should be encouraged to discuss the statements and why they agree or disagree with them.

---

because the stories have a happy ending

---

because they remind her that what Muhammad (pbuh) said is still very important

---

because they show that Muhammad (pbuh) had been given authority by Allah (God)

---

because her mum likes the stories too

---

because they show that Muhammad (pbuh) was a perfect human being

---

because she likes the way the Muslim teachers at the mosque tell the stories

---

because they remind her that Muhammad (pbuh) is very important to Muslims

---

*Figure 5.8 Why does Fatima like the stories about Muhammad (pbuh) showing authority?*

Return to page 88 for Steps 4 and 5 to complete the cycle of learning.

## Authority in Sikhism

The children should explore Step 1 in the book (pages 82–84) before they engage with Steps 2 and 3 in this section. This should then be followed by Steps 4 and 5 in the book (page 88).

### *Step 2 Contextualise*

### How did Guru Nanak show his *authority*?

- Teacher could use a picture of a Sikh child (see CD artwork F) or a Sikh persona doll  (see page 6), called Amjid (or other name), to explore this aspect of the learning. Teacher can say, 'Amjid has some stories about someone with *authority*. Shall we find out about him?'
  - ○ When Amjid and his friends go to the gurdwara they hear the songs of Guru Nanak. His mum and dad tell him about Guru Nanak at home too.
  - ○ Amjid loves hearing stories about Guru Nanak. He was very kind and good to people. Guru Nanak taught people about how God wants them to behave. The stories remind Amjid that Guru Nanak had *authority*.
  - ○ Amjid's mum and dad say that Guru Nanak had *authority* and so did the other Gurus after him. All the gurus were great teachers.
  - ○ Amjid's mum and dad say that all the *authority* from Guru Nanak is in the very special book, the Guru Granth Sahib.
- Teacher should tell the stories below (also see CD) about Guru Nanak showing *authority*. Telling the stories on consecutive days would be effective, with time allowed for reinforcement activities.
- After each story discuss some key points with the class.

---

### Questions to prompt discussion

- Do you think that Amjid and other Sikhs like this story? Why? Why not?
- Which part of the story do you think Amjid likes best?
- Which part of the story shows that Guru Nanak has *authority,* do you think?
- Why did Guru Nanak have *authority*, do you think? Show and remind the children of the list in Step 1 (page 83) about why some people have *authority* ('because they are old, because they are clever', and so on).

---

- Children can act out each story.
- Use the stories for literacy work.
- Children create a frieze or sequence pictures to illustrate each story.
- Children can complete the drawing/writing frame below (see CD)

### Guru Nanak throws water (see CD artwork 30)

Many years ago lived a great teacher called Nanak. Very wise and clever teachers were called gurus, so the people called him Guru Nanak. He had spent all his life thinking about God and asking people about God and learning about God. Guru Nanak was close to God and wanted to tell others about God. He wanted to tell people about how God wanted them to live good lives, to be kind and to share what they have with others.

Nanak went on great long journeys to tell people about how to live and it was on one of these journeys that he came across some men throwing water at the sun.

'What are you doing?' asked Guru Nanak. They explained that they believed that when people died they went to live near the sun. The men were throwing water to people who had died.

Straight away Guru Nanak picked up a bucket of water and started throwing water in the opposite direction, away from the sun.

'What are you doing, Guru Nanak?' the men asked him.

'Well,' answered Nanak, 'my farm is many miles in this direction. It is very dry and needs watering, so I am throwing water for the plants growing on my farm.'

The men were very surprised. 'The water won't get as far as your farm!' they all shouted. 'It is too far away.'

'Well, if the water can reach people near the sun, then surely it will reach my farm which is not nearly so far,' replied Guru Nanak.

The men realised how silly they had been, and that Guru Nanak had authority. They bowed down to him and listened to what he had to teach them.

### Guru Nanak is taken prisoner

Guru Nanak lived many years ago. He loved God very much and wanted to teach other people about God. He travelled around the country doing this. With him was his good friend who could play beautiful music. Nanak would sing to the people and they all came to listen to him and learn about God.

In one place the king was worried about Guru Nanak causing trouble, so he ordered that Guru Nanak and his friend be put in prison.

Now this king had been quite mean and cruel, and had attacked different towns and killed many people. Guru Nanak knew this, so when he was in prison he sang songs about the bad things that the king had done. One of the soldiers then went to the king and told him about the songs, so the king sent for Guru Nanak.

When the king met Guru Nanak he could see straight away what a good, clever, kind man he was. He could see that Guru Nanak had authority to tell people how to live good lives. The king was very sorry for all that he had done and he asked Guru Nanak to forgive him. He then set Guru Nanak and his friend free to carry on with their journey and telling people about God.

### Sajjan the robber

Many years ago lived a mean and wicked man called Sajjan. He owned a guest house where travellers would come and stay. If they were rich, he would rob them of all their money, kill them and throw them down the well. How mean is that?

One day Guru Nanak arrived at Sajjan's guest house. Guru Nanak had been travelling with his friend and they had been telling people about God and singing songs to them to teach them about how to live good lives. Nanak and his friend were very tired.

Sajjan asked Guru Nanak if he wanted to go into the guest house to sleep, but Guru Nanak showed his authority. He said that he would like to sing a special song for God and then they could dream about God.

Sajjan listened to the song and realised that Guru Nanak knew about his wicked ways. Sajjan was so sorry about his wickedness that he fell at Guru Nanak's feet and asked to be forgiven. Sajjan then gave away all his money to the poor and started to live a good life. Guru Nanak's authority had changed Sajjan's life.

This is a story that Sikhs tell. It shows them that Guru Nanak had authority.

Picture

*Figure 5.9*

### *Step 3 Evaluate*

### Is it important for Sikhs that Guru Nanak has *authority*?

- Teacher should ask the children to imagine what it would be like if each of the stories had a different ending.

**Questions to prompt discussion**

- What if the men who were throwing the water at the sun had said that they did not want to listen to Guru Nanak or that they didn't care what he said? Would the story show Guru Nanak's *authority*?
- What if the King had met Guru Nanak and thrown him straight back into prison? Would that show that Guru Nanak had *authority*?
- What if Sajjan had carried on robbing and killing people after he had met Guru Nanak? Would that story show Guru Nanak's *authority* then?
- Would Amjid and other Sikhs like to hear those stories if they did not show that Guru Nanak had *authority*? Why? Why not?
- What would Amjid and other Sikhs think about Guru Nanak if he had not shown *authority*?
- Why do you think that Amjid and other Sikhs like to hear those stories about Guru Nanak showing his *authority*?

⊙ ● Teacher should duplicate the cards provided below (and on CD). The children sort them into groups of statements that they agree or disagree with, or perhaps select three or four cards that they agree with most. The children work in pairs or threes. There are no correct or incorrect responses here, but the children should be encouraged to discuss the statements and why they agree or disagree with them.

| because the stories have a happy ending |
| --- |

| because he likes the pictures that go with the stories |
| --- |

| because they remind him that Guru Nanak helped people |
| --- |

| because they show that Guru Nanak could tell people about God |
| --- |

| because his mum likes the stories too |
| --- |

| because they show that Guru Nanak was very clever |
| --- |

| because they remind him that Guru Nanak is very important to Sikhs |
| --- |

*Figure 5.9a  Why does Amjid like the stories about Guru Nanak's authority?*

Return to page 88 for Steps 4 and 5 to complete the cycle of learning.

## Resources on the CD

### Figures

5.1   Cards – who has authority?
5.2   Cards – what gives people authority
5.3   Writing frame – *I think authority means*
5.4   Writing frame – *Jesus had authority*
5.5   Cards – Stories about Jesus showing his authority
5.6   Writing frame – *Buddha had authority*
5.6a  Cards – Stories about the Buddha showing his authority
5.7   Writing frame – *Muhammad (pbuh) had authority*
5.8   Cards – Stories about Muhammad (pbuh) showing his authority
5.9   Writing frame – *Guru Nanak had authority*
5.9a  Cards – Stories about Guru Nanak having authority

### Artwork

A.   Joe, a Christian boy
B.   Elsa, a Buddhist girl
E.   Fatima, a Muslim girl
F.   Amjid, a Sikh boy
E1–E8 cards of people with and without authority
27.  Jesus has authority over the storm
28.  Prince Siddhartha with his teachers
29.  The Kabah
30.  Guru Nanak throws water

### Stories: Christian

*Jesus shows his authority in the temple*
*Jesus has authority over the fishermen*
*Jesus has authority over the storm*

### Stories: Buddhist

*The Buddha and Mara*
*The Buddha and the messengers*
*The Buddha's wisdom*

### Stories: Muslim

*The fire at the Kabah*
*Muhammad (pbuh) spreads the message*
*Muhammad (pbuh) leads an army*

### Stories: Sikh

*Guru Nanak throws water*
*Guru Nanak is taken prisoner*
*Sajjan the robber*

# Storytelling

*Storytelling* is familiar territory for young children. This unit aims to illustrate for children *storytelling* as a particular form of expression. It is that skill that some of the great religious leaders used to convey their messages and their teachings, and that members of religious traditions continue to use. *Storytelling* is the concept or key idea in focus, so the children will need to engage with some stories in order to consider the purpose of the *storytelling*. A number of stories are provided in this unit.

Exploring the concept of *storytelling* can form the foundation for the concepts of *interpretation* or *messages* at Key Stage 2. The book explores the concept within a Christian context through the example of how Jesus used *storytelling*. The concept of *storytelling* is also explored within aspects of other major religions.

How did the Buddha use *storytelling*?
How do Hindus use *storytelling*?
How do Jews use *storytelling*?
How do Muslims use *storytelling*?
How do Sikhs use *storytelling*?

**COMMUNICATE (1)**
What is our experience of storytelling?

**APPLY (2)**
How does storytelling affect us and others?

**ENQUIRE (3)**
What does storytelling mean?

**CONTEXTUALISE (4)**
How did religious leaders and how do religious traditions use storytelling?

**EVALUATE (5)**
Is it important for religious leaders and religious traditions to use storytelling?

## Storytelling in Christianity

### *Step 1 Communicate*

#### What is our experience of *storytelling*?

● The teacher reminds the children of some stories they have heard in class. Ask them to decide which they liked and share their choices.

● Send a note home to parents to ask that the children bring in favourite stories to share and discuss. Can the children be storytellers?

● Explain to the class that stories can be in books, on television, on radio or told by people – storytellers. Which way do they prefer to hear a story?

● The teacher wears a storyteller's hat or badge and tells a story, then distributes the story in simple text to be read. Which do the children prefer?

---

### Questions to prompt discussion

● Do you know anyone who is a storyteller? Can anyone be a storyteller?
● Who is your favourite storyteller? Why?
● How does *storytelling* make you feel?
● When do you like to listen to a storyteller?
● Have you ever been a storyteller?
● How did that feel?

---

● The children talk about *storytelling* in circle time.
● Invite a storyteller into class to tell a story (no book reading!).
● Make a storyteller badge or hat to be worn by the child or adult telling the story.

### *Step 2 Apply*

#### How does *storytelling* affect us and others?

● Place the six pictures below (also see CD Figure 6.1) on a separate table. The children are given one or two counters. The children can look at all the pictures and then place their counters on the picture or pictures that show when they most like to hear some *storytelling*. The teacher can count up the 'votes' and discuss the children's responses.

● Have a class discussion focussing on the questions below.

## Questions to prompt discussion

- Do you always like listening to storytellers? Why? Why not?
- Would you want to hear a storyteller if you were in the middle of playing on the computer, or out on your bike? Why? Why not?
- Is *storytelling* a good way of learning? Why? Why not?
- Is it a good way of learning everything? Always?
- Would *storytelling* help you to learn how to skateboard? Why? Why not?
- Does *storytelling* always make you feel happy?
- What if the story is very sad?
- What if the storyteller says something you don't want to hear? How do you feel then?
- What if the storyteller told you a story that made you feel silly or angry? What would you do?

*Figure 6.1*

### *Step 3 Enquire*

**What does *storytelling* mean?**

In this element of learning the children are exploring the characteristics of *storytelling*.

- In pairs or groups the children select words and phrases from the list below (also on CD) that they think 'go with' the word '*storytelling*'.
- Compare words as a class and discuss agreements and disagreements.
- Display the final list and add any of the children's own ideas.

The teacher can duplicate and cut up cards below (see CD Figure 6.2) for the children to use in this activity. Which words go with the word '*storytelling*'?

Which words go with the word 'storytelling'?

| | |
|---|---|
| interesting | reading |
| make you listen | funny |
| lots of pictures | make you look |
| sad | lots of writing |
| boring | help you to remember |
| not from a book | exciting |
| from a book | make you feel silly |

*Figure 6.2*

### *Step 4 Contextualise*

**How did Jesus use *storytelling*?**

- The teacher could use a picture of a Christian child (see CD artwork A) or use a Christian persona doll (see page 6), called Joe, for example, to explore this aspect of the learning. The teacher can say, 'Joe knows about someone who was a very important storyteller. Shall we find out about him?'

○ When Joe goes to church with his mum he hears about Jesus. The stories about Jesus are in the Bible, the special book for Christians. Jesus was a very good sto-ryteller and some of the stories he told are in the Bible.

○ Joe thinks that Jesus was very clever. He told stories to help people to understand things better.

○ Joe really likes the stories. Sometimes his mum tells him some of the stories at home.

○ Joe says that Jesus must have been a very good storyteller because hundreds of people used to go and listen to him. His stories made them think hard.

○ When Joe goes to Sunday school in the church, the Sunday school teacher tells the children stories that Jesus told. Sometimes they sing songs about the stories and sometimes they draw pictures.

- Show the picture of Jesus telling stories to a crowd (see CD artwork 31).
- The teacher becomes the storyteller in order to tell the three stories below (also on CD) that Jesus told. Telling each story on consecutive days would be effective, with time allowed for reinforcement activities.
- After each story the class discuss some key points.

> **Questions to prompt discussion**
>
> - Do you think Joe and other Christians like this story? Why? Why not?
> - Which part of the story do you think Joe likes best?
> - Why do you think Jesus told this story?
> - What do you think Jesus wanted the people to learn from this story?

- The children can act out each story.
- Use the stories for literacy work.
- Children create a frieze or sequence pictures to illustrate each story.
- Children can retell one of the stories to a partner or a group, or complete the drawing/ writing frame (see CD Figure 6.5).
- Children draw pictures of Jesus telling stories.
- In pairs or small groups the children take it in turns to be the storyteller, or different children in the class can be the storyteller for different parts of the story.
- Teacher explains that Jesus told stories to help people understand things better. One day Jesus had said: 'Love other people as much as you love yourself.' One person did not understand and said to Jesus, 'What do you mean, "love other people"? Who are the "other people" I should love?' This is the story Jesus told to help him understand. Teacher tells the story (wearing the *storytelling* hat or badge).

### The good Samaritan

A man was on a journey. Some robbers beat him up and took all his things away. They left him half-dead in the road.

A little bit later a priest came along the road, but he did not stop and help the man. He kept on walking.

Another man came along. He looked at the man who had been beaten up, and then walked off and left him.

Then another man came along the road. When he saw the poor man who had been beaten up he felt very sorry for him. He went over to him, cleaned his cuts and put bandages on him. Then he helped him onto the animal he had been riding. He took him to a hotel and looked after him.

The next day he gave the hotel owner some money and said, 'Look after this man. When I come back this way I will pay you the rest of the money you may need to spend on him.'

When Jesus had finished telling the story he said to the man who had asked him the question: 'So who was the friend to the man who had been beaten up?'

'The man who had been kind,' said the man.

Then Jesus said, 'You go and do the same.'

- Discuss the story (prompt questions are on page 106).
- Introduce the next story below by saying, 'Jesus sometimes told people stories to help them to understand how to behave better and to be better people.' The teacher then tells the story.

### The clever man and the silly man

One day Jesus said, 'If people do what I tell them to do they will be like the clever man in the story.

A clever man built his house on rock. Then the rain poured down. The rivers became very full and flooded the land. The wind blew hard against the house and it rained and rained. But the house did not fall down. The house was strong, because it had been built on rock.'

Jesus said, 'If people hear what I say and don't do what I have told them, then they are like the silly man.

A silly man built a house on sand. Then the rain poured down. The rivers became very full and flooded the land. The wind blew hard against the house. The house fell down. What a terrible fall that was!'

- Discuss the story (prompt questions are on page 106).
- Reinforce the story using the activities suggested on page 106.
- Teacher introduces another story. 'Jesus told some stories to help people to know what God is like.' Teacher tells the story below (wearing the *storytelling* hat or badge).

### The man who lost his sheep

There was once a man who looked after lots of sheep. In fact he had one hundred sheep to look after. He would count them every now and again to make sure that they were all safe.

One day the man got very worried. One of his sheep was missing. What could have happened to it? He left all the other sheep behind and went off to look for that sheep. He looked high and low, behind bushes, behind rocks. He kept on and on looking and did not give up.

At last he found the lost sheep. He was so pleased! He carried the sheep on his shoulders and went back. When he saw his friends the man called to them. 'Look! I lost my sheep and now I have found it. I think we should celebrate.'

● Discuss the story with the class (prompt questions are on page 106).
● Reinforce the story using the activities suggested on page 106.

### *Step 5 Evaluate*

### Was it important for Jesus to use *storytelling*?

**Questions to prompt discussion**

● Do you think that, *storytelling* was a good way for Jesus to teach the people?
● What other way could he use?
● If he had handed out papers or books for people to read would that have been so good? Why? Why not?
● Would the people have learned as much?
● Is it still useful to hear Jesus' stories? Why? Why not?
● Do we think Jesus was a good storyteller?
● How do we know?
● What difference did his *storytelling* make?
● What would have happened if he had been no good at telling stories?

● Use the whiteboard or print on A4 sheets of paper the following statements for discussion (see Figure 6.4 and CD). Ask the children what they might say in each column. It may be helpful to provide the prompts below (see Figure 6.3 and CD) for the children to consider and place on the charts. The children could consider and place their own ideas on the charts.

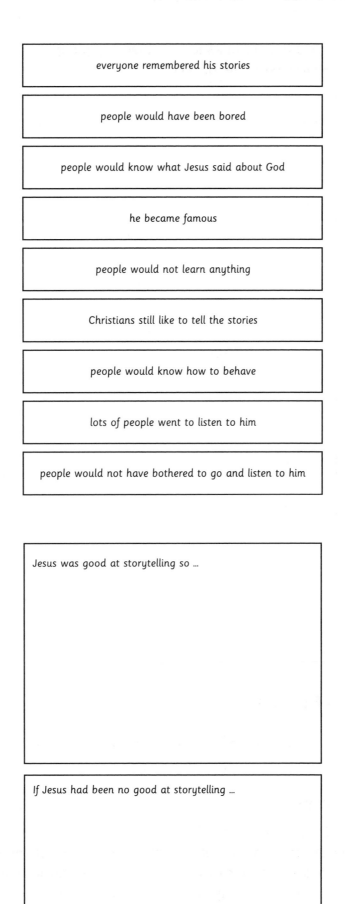

everyone remembered his stories

people would have been bored

people would know what Jesus said about God

he became famous

people would not learn anything

Christians still like to tell the stories

people would know how to behave

lots of people went to listen to him

people would not have bothered to go and listen to him

*Figure 6.3*

Jesus was good at storytelling so …

If Jesus had been no good at storytelling …

*Figure 6.4*

● The children tell one of the stories to a partner or a group, or complete the writing/
drawing frame below (see Figure 6.5 and CD).

Name ..............................................................................

Jesus told stories because

...............................................................................

...............................................................................

...............................................................................

...............................................................................

Here is a story Jesus told.

*Figure 6.5*

## Storytelling in Buddhism

The children should explore Steps 1, 2 and 3 in the book (pages 103–105) before they engage with Steps 4 and 5 in this section.

### *Step 4 Contextualise*

### How did the Buddha use *storytelling*?

● The teacher could use a picture of a Buddhist child (see CD artwork B) or use a Buddhist persona doll (see page 6), called Elsa, for example, to explore this aspect of the learning. The teacher can say that Elsa knows about someone who was a good storyteller.

○ Elsa loves to hear about the Buddha.

○ He lived a long time ago, but he told stories that are still important to Buddhists.

○ When Elsa goes to the temple with her friends, the monks (the men who live at the temple and teach people about the Buddha) sometimes tell them stories that the Buddha told.

- ○ The monks say the Buddha was very clever. Many people went to him to learn about what to do and how to live, and he helped them by telling them stories.
  - ○ The monks say that the Buddha was such a great and good teacher that all the stories he told are still important for them today.
  - ○ They say he is the most important teacher that there could ever be.
- Show an image of the Buddha telling stories (see CD artwork 32).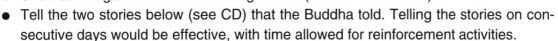
- Tell the two stories below (see CD) that the Buddha told. Telling the stories on consecutive days would be effective, with time allowed for reinforcement activities.
- After each story discuss some key points.

---

**Questions to prompt discussion**

- Do you think that Elsa and other Buddhists like this story? Why? Why not?
- Which part of the story do you think Elsa likes best?
- Why do you think the Buddha told this story?
- What do you think the Buddha wanted to teach people when he told this story?

---

- The children can act out each story.
- Use the stories for literacy work.
- Children create a frieze or sequence pictures to illustrate each story.
- Children can retell one of the stories to a partner or a group, or complete the drawing/ writing frame (see CD Figure 6.6).

Note: Buddhism is enormously diverse. Some Buddhist traditions tell different versions and interpretations of these stories. The stories have more significance within the beliefs and practices of some traditions than others. The story of the blind men and the elephant is ascribed to various religious traditions, but many Buddhists claim that it was told by the Buddha.

**The blind men and the elephant**

In a land far away was a great city, and in the great city was an emperor, and the emperor had some men to help him rule the land. But the emperor was fed up with his helpers. They were always arguing and squabbling. 'I am right about this!' 'No, you are not. I am right in this situation!' they would say, day after day, about everything. The emperor decided to teach them a lesson.

He called all his helpers to the courtyard. There, in the courtyard, was an elephant. Then the emperor brought in five blind men from the street. He stood them around the elephant and asked them what was in front of them.

Well, the first man went up and felt the elephant's head. 'This is a great big pot,' said the first man.

The second man went up and felt the elephant's ears. 'No, this is a big fan.'

The third man went up to the elephant and came across its leg. 'This is a tree,' he exclaimed as he felt the elephant's great big leg covered in rough skin, like the bark of a tree.

The fourth man went forward and got hold of the elephant's trunk, which wriggled about in his hand. He quickly let go. 'Ugh! It's a snake,' he shouted.

The last blind man made his way forward and felt the elephant's tail, which was long and thin with lots of wiry hairs on the end. 'This is a brush,' he declared.

Then the blind men all started to argue about what they had felt. 'It's a brush!' 'No, it's not. It's a tree!' 'It's nothing like a tree. It's a fan!' And so on and on they went. Each man had only felt a small part of the whole animal.

The emperor looked at his helpers. 'You are just like those blind men. You only see one part of a problem and each one of you thinks that you are right. That does not help me rule my kingdom.'

## The five travellers

Many, many years ago there lived a wise old man. He was a great teacher, and he had five young men who would come and learn from him. In time the old man became very frail and he knew that he would soon die.

One day he brought the five young men together and told them that, after his death, he would like them to go to the city where he had been born. He asked if they would say prayers for him when they got there. Even though the city was many, many miles away, they all agreed.

Some time after that the old man died. The young men were very sad and were all determined to do as the old man had asked, so they set off to the city where the old man had been born.

They travelled along together for a while, until one of the young men got fed up with the others. 'You are going too slowly!' he said. 'I want to get there quickly and then get on with my life.' The others told him to go on ahead, which he did. He rushed along, barely giving himself enough time to eat or sleep, and he was the first to arrive at the city.

Another one of the group found that the others were walking a bit too fast for him. 'I am getting really tired,' he said. 'You go ahead. I'll see you later.' He stopped to rest under a tree and fell asleep. That night he had a good meal in a village and a good night's rest and carried on his walk. The others were well ahead now, so each day he walked by himself for a few miles and then rested. He carried on doing this for a whole year, but he got to the city in the end. He kept his promise to the old man.

The other three men were walking on together to the city, when one of them got worried. 'Are we on the right road?' he said. He asked someone in a field which way to go, and this man sent him off in another direction. 'I'm going this way!' he shouted to his two companions. And he did. He kept asking different people which way to go, and in the end he walked miles and miles in a roundabout route. He did get to the city in the end, but it took him two years.

Now there were two young men walking together. One of them had not listened very well to all that the wise old teacher had taught him. He soon got tired of the journey. He was hungry, his feet hurt and he was fed up with having no money. 'I'm going home,' he announced, and he turned on his heel and headed back to where he had come from.

When he got home he wanted to get money quickly. He started stealing, and was caught and thrown into prison. When he was released he carried on stealing. This happened again and again. He just did not learn. Then he started to drink and take drugs until he became very ill and the doctor told him that he must change his ways or he would die. Many years had passed since this young man had made his promise to his old teacher. He suddenly remembered his promise. 'I must go to that city,' the young man thought. So this time he did. It was a long, long time since he had first set off, but he completed the journey in the end.

There was one young man left walking along the road to the city, and we do not yet know what happened to him. He kept on walking and kept up a good pace. One day, however, he came across a man carrying a huge pile of wood which was so heavy it was weighing him down. This young man was a good, kind young man, and he felt so sorry for the man carrying the wood that he offered to help. He carried some of the wood to the man's village, which was many miles away. When he got there, there was so much work to do that he offered to help with that too.

After some time he carried on with his journey to the city, but then he met someone else who needed help. He was such a kind young man that he always stopped to help. Time and time again he stopped to help before carrying on his journey. He helped so many people that his journey took him ten years. But the young man kept his promise to his wise old teacher and reached the city in the end.

- Discuss each story (prompt questions are on page 111).
- Reinforce each story using the activities suggested on page 111.
- Children can retell one of the stories to a partner or a group, or complete the writing/ drawing frame (see Figure 6.6 and CD).

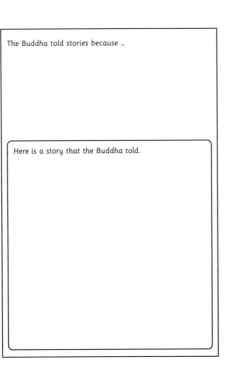

The Buddha told stories because …

Here is a story that the Buddha told.

*Figure 6.6*

## *Step 5 Evaluate*

## Was it important for the Buddha to use *storytelling*?

> **Questions to prompt discussion**
>
> - Do you think that *storytelling* was a good way for the Buddha to teach the people?
> - What other way could he use?
> - If he had handed out papers or books for people to read would that have been so good? Why? Why not?
> - Would the people have learned as much?
> - Is it still useful to hear the Buddha's stories? Why? Why not?
> - Do we think that the Buddha was a good storyteller?
> - How do we know?
> - What difference did his *storytelling* make?
> - What would have happened if he had been no good at telling stories?

- Use the whiteboard or print on A4 sheets of paper the following statements for discussion (see Figure 6.8 and CD). Ask the children what they might say in each column. Provide the prompts below (see Figure 6.7 and CD) for the children to consider and place on the charts.

> everyone remembered his stories

> people would have been bored

> people would not learn much

> Buddhists still like to tell the stories

> people would know how to behave

> lots of people went to listen to him

> people would not have bothered to go and listen to him

> he made people think about important things in life

*Figure 6.7*

The Buddha was good at storytelling so ...

If the Buddha had been no good at storytelling ...

*Figure 6.8*

## Storytelling in Hinduism

The children should explore Steps 1, 2 and 3 in the book (pages 103–105) before they engage with Steps 4 and 5 in this section.

### *Step 4 Contextualise*

### How do Hindus use *storytelling*?
- The teacher could use a picture of a Hindu child (see CD artwork D) or a Hindu  persona doll (see page 6), called Sita, for example, to explore this aspect of the learning. Explain that Sita loves to hear storytellers.
  - ○ Sita loves to hear her granny who is a very good storyteller.
  - ○ Sita's granny tells her all sorts of stories about how powerful God is.
  - ○ Sometimes Sita's granny tells her stories when it is a special celebration and sometimes she just tells stories because they help Sita to understand about God.
- The teacher should show the image of a Hindu telling stories (see CD artwork 33).
- The teacher should tell the two Hindu stories below (see CD). Telling the stories on consecutive days would be effective, with time allowed for reinforcement activities.
- After each story discuss some key points with the class.

**Questions to prompt discussion**

- Do you think that Sita and other Hindus like this story? Why? Why not?
- Which part of the story do you think Sita likes best?
- Why do you think Hindus tell this story?
- What do you think Hindus want to teach people when they tell this story?

- The children can act out each story.
- Use the stories for literacy work.
- Children create a frieze or sequence pictures to illustrate each story.

- Children can retell one of the stories to a partner or a group, or complete the drawing/ writing frame. (See CD Figure 6.9)

### Lord Krishna protects all the people

In a land far, far away lived the wonderful Lord Krishna. He was good and kind and everyone loved him.

In that land it was time for a special festival, and Lord Krishna said that all the people should be happy at festival time. He told the people that, at festival time, they should think about all the good things they had, like the cows that give delicious milk and butter, the trees that give wonderful fruits and provide shade when it is hot, and the beautiful mountain where these things live and grow.

The people were really pleased with this idea, and when the day of the festival came they all dressed in their finest clothes and put flowers in their hair. They scrubbed and decorated the cows with bells and pretty colours. All was ready and they made a happy procession, going up the mountain with Lord Krishna.

When they got to the top they said prayers of thanks for all the good things. They said prayers to Krishna, to the mountain, to the trees and to the cows. They ate wonderful food and sang songs, and all the people were happy. But they were also tired. It was nearly night time, so they found comfortable places on the mountain to settle down and sleep.

Now, Indra, the king of all the Gods, had been watching. He became very jealous of all the fuss that was being made about Krishna, the trees, the mountain and the cows. He thought that the people ought to be praying to him instead. 'I'll show them,' he thought. Indra decided that he would make trouble. He made the wind blow, and it became colder and colder. Then the thunder rumbled, and gradually a terrible storm started to rage. Indra made the rain poor down on all the people on the mountain. They were very frightened.

Krishna felt so sorry for the people, and he led them to a cave. They moved rocks and stones so that they could all go in and be protected from the terrible storm. But then something dreadful happened. Indra made the ground shudder and shake, and the top of the mountain started to break away. The people were terrified.

A truly amazing thing happened next. Krishna was so powerful that he held up the top of the mountain over the heads of the people. They were all under the mountain top, protected from the storm. Everyone was so pleased about what Krishna had done that they started to sing. Then the rain stopped, the wind stopped and the sun came out.

Krishna led the people down the mountain, and as they went he told them that they should not be frightened of Indra any more. They could all pray to Indra and thank him for the wonderful rain that makes everything grow.

## Krishna and the buttermilk

When Lord Krishna was very young he really loved the creamy taste of buttermilk.

One day his mother had some really creamy buttermilk in a large jug. 'Don't you touch the buttermilk, Krishna,' she said, and she placed the jug on a very high shelf way out of Krishna's reach.

Now, Krishna really, really loved buttermilk. He looked around the room and started to see how he could reach the jug and taste that gorgeous buttermilk. He dragged cushions across the room and piled them up so that he was able to crawl up and reach the jug. In went his finger and into his mouth went the gorgeous buttermilk. Yum yum!

Then the door opened and in came Krishna's mother. 'Oh Krishna,' she whispered. 'Have you been eating the buttermilk?' Baby Krishna shook his head, but his mother gently took hold of his chin and opened up his mouth. When she looked into his mouth she was really amazed. She could not see any buttermilk, but she could see the whole universe. She could see the sky, the sun, the moon and all the stars. What an amazing baby Krishna was.

- Discuss each story with the class (prompt questions are on page 114).
- Reinforce each story using the activities suggested on page 114.
- Children can retell one of the stories to a partner or a group, or complete the writing/drawing frame. (See Figure 6.9 and CD)

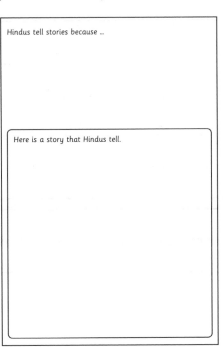

*Figure 6.9*

## Step 5 Evaluate

### Is it important for Hindus to use *storytelling*?

**Questions to prompt discussion**

- Do you think that *storytelling* is a good way for Hindus to teach people?
- What other way could be used?
- If they had handed out papers or books for people to read would that be so good? Why? Why not?
- Would Hindus learn as much?
- What difference does *storytelling* make to Hindus?

- Use the whiteboard or print on A4 sheets of paper the following statements for discussion (see Figure 6.11 and CD). Ask the children what they might say in each column. Provide the prompts below (see Figure 6.10 and CD) for the children to consider and place their own ideas on the charts.

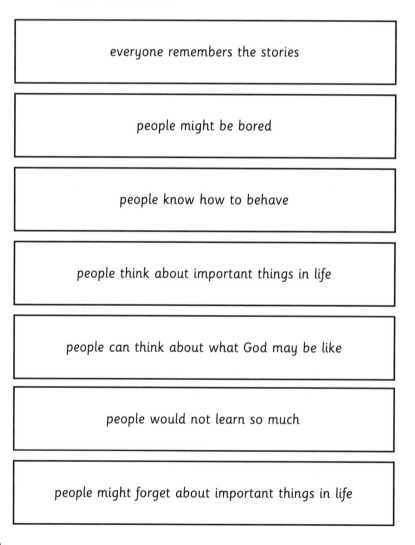

everyone remembers the stories

people might be bored

people know how to behave

people think about important things in life

people can think about what God may be like

people would not learn so much

people might forget about important things in life

*Figure 6.10*

Figure 6.11

## Storytelling in Judaism

The children should explore Steps 1, 2 and 3 in the book (pages 103–105) before they engage with Steps 4 and 5 in this section.

### *Step 4 Contextualise*

### How do Jews use *storytelling*?

- The teachers could use a picture of a Jewish child (see CD artwork C) or a Jewish persona doll (see page 6), called Joshua, for example, to explore this aspect of the learning. The teacher should tell the children that Joshua loves to hear storytellers.
  - ○ Joshua loves to hear stories about Jewish people who lived a long, long time ago.
  - ○ Joshua says the stories help him to think about how God has always helped the Jewish people.
  - ○ Joshua thinks *storytelling* is very important. When there is a special celebration or a festival there is usually some *storytelling* too.
  - ○ Joshua's dad tells Jewish stories when they are having special meals. He's a great storyteller.
  - ○ Joshua's mum tells him stories before he goes to sleep at night.

(▶) ● The teacher should show an image of a Jewish father telling stories (see CD artwork 35).

(▶) ● The teacher should tell the two Jewish stories below (see CD). Telling the stories on consecutive days would be effective, with time allowed for reinforcement activities.

● After each story discuss some key points with the class.

---

### Questions to prompt discussion

● Do you think that Joshua and other Jews like this story? Why? Why not?
● Which part of the story do you think Joshua likes best?
● Why do you think Jews tell this story?
● What do you think Jews want to teach people when they tell this story?

---

● The children can act out each story.
● Use the stories for literacy work.
● Children create a frieze or sequence pictures to illustrate each story.

(▶) ● Children can retell one of the stories to a partner or a group, or complete the drawing/ writing frame. (See CD Figure 6.12)

---

### The story of Esther

There was once a huge kingdom and it was ruled by a great and powerful king. Now, the king had a helper who thought a lot of himself. His name was Haman. He thought he was so important that as he walked around he would shout at people to bow down in front of him. Everyone was a bit scared of Haman, so they did bow down when he went past them. He liked it when they did that!

One day, however, the puffed-up Haman came across someone who would not bow down in front of him. His name was Mordecai. Mordecai was a Jew. Mordecai loved God very much and did not want to bow down in front of anyone except God. Mordecai said that nobody could be as important as God.

Now, this made Haman absolutely furious. How dare anyone refuse to bow down in front of him? So off he went to the king. 'I have come across someone who diso-beys me, your majesty,' he said. 'He is a Jew and he and all the other Jews in the land always try to disobey the laws. I think you should have him killed, your majesty. I think all the other Jews should be killed too.' Without thinking about it too much, the king agreed.

When Mordecai heard the news that he and all the Jews would be killed he knew that something should be done. He went to find his beautiful cousin Esther. Esther was the queen of that land. She was married to the king. Esther was a Jew too, but the king did not know this.

Mordecai pleaded with her. 'Please go to the king and ask him to change his order to kill all the Jews.'

Now, Esther knew that this was a dangerous thing to do. The king might get very angry with her and punish her, but she knew that she had to try and save all the Jews.

So Esther gathered up all her courage and went to see the king. The king was really pleased to see her. 'Esther, whatever you want you can have. What is your request?'

Esther told the king about what had happened. 'Please take back your order to kill all the Jewish people. I am a Jew too. I would die with all the other Jews.'

The king was horrified with all that Esther had told him. He was so cross about the way that the wicked Haman had been so mean to the Jewish people. As punishment the king ordered that Haman should be killed. Then the king made Mordecai, the Jew, his helper instead of the wicked Haman. All the Jews had been saved because Esther had been so brave.

## David and Goliath

Many hundreds of years ago there was a large army of soldiers called Philistines. They were planning to attack the Jewish people. The Philistines stood on one side of a valley, getting ready for the attack. The Jews were very scared, but they also had an army, of Jewish soldiers. The Jewish soldiers stood on the other side of the valley, facing the Philistine soldiers, waiting to fight back.

Every day the Philistines sent out their biggest soldier, Goliath. He was massive! He was nearly 3 metres tall, and was covered in armour. He wore a helmet and he carried a great spear. There he would stand, at the other side of the valley, and shout, in his booming voice, to the Jewish soldiers. 'What are you all doing standing there?' he shouted. 'Send one of your men to fight me. If he beats me we will all be your slaves. If he loses, you will be our slaves.'

The Jewish soldiers were terrified. Nobody was brave enough to fight the giant soldier Goliath.

One day a young man called David came to visit his older brothers who were in the Jewish army. He brought them food and came to see if they were well. When he was there he saw the great giant Goliath on the other side of the valley. He heard Goliath shouting, 'Send me a soldier to fight me.'

David thought that he could fight the giant soldier, but his brothers would not hear of it. 'You are only a boy and you have never been a soldier,' they said, but David felt that he could do it.

David decided to go to the king of the Jewish people and tell him that he would fight the giant Goliath. 'When I look after my father's sheep, if a bear or a lion comes, I fight them and kill them. God takes care of me when I fight lions and bears and he will help me fight the great Philistine soldier called Goliath,' David explained to the king.

The king agreed, and offered to give David some armour to protect him. But David did not like the armour. It was too big and heavy. Off he went to meet the great giant soldier with just a catapult, five stones and his stick.

David faced Goliath across the valley. Goliath roared at David. But David felt brave. He knew that God would help him. 'I will beat you, Goliath, and the whole world will know that we have a great God. Everyone here will see that God will save the Jews.'

David put one of his stones in the catapult and spun it around above his head. Suddenly the stone shot into the air and hit the great giant Goliath right on his head. Goliath fell to the ground. David ran up to Goliath, took the giant's sword from him and chopped off his head with it. The great Goliath was dead.

All the Philistines were terrified when they saw this. They turned and ran away, and they were followed by the Jewish soldiers who ran after them. God had helped David to save all the Jewish people.

- Discuss each story with the class (prompt questions are on page 120).
- Reinforce each story using the activities suggested on page 120.
- The children can retell one of the stories to a partner or a group, or complete the writing/drawing frame (see Figure 6.12 and CD).

 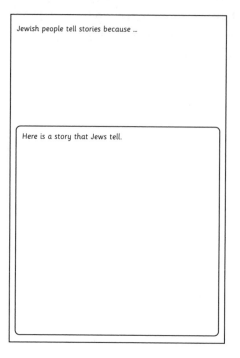

Jewish people tell stories because ...

Here is a story that Jews tell.

Figure 6.12

### Step 5 Evaluate

### Is it important for Jews to use *storytelling*?

**Questions to prompt discussion**

- Do you think that *storytelling* is a good way for Jews to teach people?
- What other way could be used?
- If they handed out papers or books for people to read would that be so good? Why? Why not?
- Would Jews learn as much?
- Would they understand so well?
- What difference does *storytelling* make to Jews?

- Use the whiteboard or print on A4 sheets of paper the following statements for discussion (see Figure 6.14 and CD). Ask the children what they might say in each column.
- Provide the prompts below (see Figure 6.13 and CD) for the children to consider and place their own ideas on the charts.

| everyone remembers the stories |
| --- |

| people might be bored |
| --- |

| people know how to behave |
| --- |

| people think about important things in life |
| --- |

| people can think about what God may be like |
| --- |

| people would not learn so much |
| --- |

| people might forget about important things in life |
| --- |

*Figure 6.13*

| Jews use storytelling so that ... |
| --- |
| |

| If Jews did not use storytelling ... |
| --- |
| |

*Figure 6.14*

## Storytelling in Islam

The children should explore Steps 1, 2 and 3 in the book (pages 103–105) before they engage with Steps 4 and 5 in this section.

### *Step 4 Contextualise*

### How do Muslims use *storytelling*?

- The teacher could use a picture of a Muslim child (see CD artwork E) or a Muslim persona doll (see page 6), called Fatima, for example, to explore this aspect of the learning. The teacher should tell the children that Fatima loves to hear storytellers.
  - ○ Fatima loves to hear stories about Muhammad (pbuh) who lived a long, long time ago. Muhammad (pbuh) was a messenger from Allah (God).
  - ○ Fatima says that the stories help her to think about how Allah wants Muslim people to behave.
  - ○ Fatima thinks that *storytelling* is very important. When there is a special celebration or a festival there is usually some *storytelling* too.
  - ○ Fatima's granddad is a great storyteller. He tells brilliant stories about Muhammad (pbuh).
  - ○ Sometimes the teacher at the mosque tells stories about things that Muhammad (pbuh) said and did. She is a good storyteller too.
- Show the image of a Muslim telling stories (see CD artwork 36).
- Teacher should tell the two Muslim stories below. (See CD) Telling the stories on consecutive days would be effective, with time allowed for reinforcement activities.
- After each story discuss some key points.

> ### Questions to prompt discussion
>
> - Do you think that Fatima and other Muslims like to hear this story? Why? Why not?
> - Which part of the story do you think Fatima likes best?
> - Why do you think Muslims tell this story?
> - What do you think Muslims want to teach people when they tell this story?

- Use the stories for literacy work.
- The children can retell one of the stories to a partner or a group, or complete the writing frame (see CD Figure 6.15).

Note: There are no images of Muhammad (pbuh) in Islam, and it would be inappropriate for the children to act out the stories or produce any pictures of Muhammad (pbuh). Some Muslim children may not wish to draw any human form.

## Muhammad (pbuh) at the stream

Many years ago lived a wonderful, good, kind man called Muhammad (pbuh). Muhammad (pbuh) was Allah's special messenger and he would teach people how to behave well, and how to do what Allah wants.

One day Muhammad (pbuh) was walking with some friends and they were all hot and tired. Then they came to a stream so they decided to stop and cool themselves. The friends all rushed into the water. They splashed about and they threw water at each other. They ran through the water so that it became rather muddy, but it was lovely and cool.

Suddenly they noticed that Muhammad (pbuh) was not joining in. He had taken a small bowl from his bag and he gently dipped the bowl into the stream to collect some water. Then he carefully washed his hands and his feet using the water in the bowl.

His friends were very puzzled. 'There is plenty of water in the stream. Why are you filling the bowl?' they asked him.

Muhammad (pbuh) explained. He said that Allah has given the wonderful gift of water. There is plenty of water for everyone, but even so, no small part of that wonderful gift should be wasted.

## Muhammad (pbuh) has rubbish thrown at him

There were some people in the land where Muhammad (pbuh) lived who did not agree with the things he said. 'Who does he think he is, telling us how we should behave?' they would say.

There was one particular old woman who was very cross about the things Muhammad (pbuh) said. In fact, she was so cross with him that she would throw rubbish over him every time he walked past her house. Muhammad (pbuh) was never angry, though. He would always look at her and greet her when she had thrown rubbish on him.

One day Muhammad (pbuh) was passing the old woman's house, but no rubbish came flying out of the widow at him. He was surprised! He decided to investigate and asked the woman's neighbours where she was. 'She is ill,' they explained, 'and she is all alone in her house.'

Muhammad (pbuh) wasted no time at all. He went straight into the old woman's house. He made a meal for the old woman, brought her some water and then cleaned the house. She was so pleased that someone had bothered to come and help her when she felt so ill. She was amazed that, even though she had been so mean to him, it was Muhammad (pbuh) who came to help her.

The old woman started to feel really sorry for the way she had treated Muhammad (pbuh). When she was well she decided that she would be a better person. She decided that she should be kind, like Muhammad (pbuh), and she became a good Muslim.

- Discuss each story with the class (prompt questions are on page 124).
- Children complete the writing frame for literacy link (see Figure 6.15 and CD), or retell ◀ the story themselves.

Muslim people tell stories because …

Here is a story that Muslims tell.

*Figure 6.15*

### Step 5 Evaluate

### Is it important for Muslims to use *storytelling*?

**Questions to prompt discussion**

- Do you think that *storytelling* is a good way for Muslims to teach people?
- What other way could be used?
- Would that be a good way to learn?
- What difference does *storytelling* make to Muslims?

- Use the whiteboard or print on A4 sheets of paper the following statements for discussion (see Figure 6.17 and CD). Ask the children what they might say in each column. You may want to provide the prompts below (see Figure 6.16 and CD) for the children to consider and place on the charts.

| everyone remembers the stories |
| --- |

| people might be bored |
| --- |

| people know how to behave |
| --- |

| people think about important things in life |
| --- |

| people can think about what Allah may be like |
| --- |

| people would not learn so much |
| --- |

| people might forget about important things in life |
| --- |

*Figure 6.16*

Muslims use storytelling so that …

If Muslims did not use storytelling …

*Figure 6.17*

## Storytelling in Sikhism

The children should explore Steps 1, 2 and 3 in the book (pages 103–105) before they engage with Steps 4 and 5 in this section.

### *Step 4 Contextualise*

#### How do Sikhs use *storytelling*?

▶ ● The teacher could use a picture of a Sikh child (see CD artwork F) or a Sikh persona doll (see page 6), called Amjid, for example, to explore this aspect of the learning. The teacher should tell the children that Amjid loves to hear storytellers.

○ Amjid loves to hear stories about Gurus who were great teachers and leaders who lived a long, long time ago.

○ Amjid says that the stories help him to think about how they should always help other people.

○ Amjid thinks that *storytelling* is very important. When there is a special celebration or a festival there is usually some *storytelling* too.

○ Amjid's granny is very good at *storytelling*. She makes him feel that he is in the story, watching the Gurus and what they did.

▶ ● Teacher should show the image of a Sikh telling stories (see CD artwork 34).

▶ ● Teacher should tell the two Sikh stories below (see CD). Telling the stories on consecutive days would be effective, with time allowed for reinforcement activities.

● After each story discuss some key points with the class.

> **Questions to prompt discussion:**
>
> ● Do you think that Amjid and other Sikhs like this story? Why? Why not?
> ● Which part of the story do you think Amjid likes best?
> ● Why do you think Sikhs tell this story?
> ● What do you think Sikhs want to teach people when they tell this story?

● Use the stories for literacy work.
● Children create a frieze or sequence pictures to illustrate each story.
▶ ● Children can retell the story to a partner or a group, or complete the drawing/writing frame (see CD Figure 6.18).

### Guru Nanak and the bowl of milk

Many years ago in a country far away lived a very wise and wonderful man called Nanak. He was an amazing teacher and many people came to listen to what he said about how they should live and how they should help each other. In that land a really, special, wise teacher is called a Guru, so they called him Guru Nanak.

Guru Nanak travelled far and wide teaching people. One day, he was about to enter a great city to teach the people, when a man came to him carrying a bowl of milk. The bowl was absolutely full to the brim with milk. The man wanted to show Guru Nanak that the city was full up, just like the bowl of milk. He said to Guru

Nanak, 'This city has plenty of holy men who can teach us. We don't need any more. There is no room for you in this city!'

Guru Nanak did a very clever thing. He picked a tiny flower which had a lovely smell. He carefully dropped it in the milk where it floated. Not a drop of milk was spilled but the milk had the wonderful perfume of the flower in it.

'Look,' said Guru Nanak. 'There is always room for a little more goodness. A small flower can perfume a bowl of milk and one man can help people to do good things and to love God.'

The man was sorry for what he had said and he welcomed Guru Nanak into the city so that he could teach the people.

### Guru Gobind Rai and the five brave men

There once lived a great leader of the Sikh people. His name was Guru Gobind Rai. One day he arranged for all the Sikh people to come to a huge gathering. He wanted everyone to meet together as he had something very important to say.

The great day came and all the Sikhs were gathered, eagerly waiting to hear what their great leader might say. In front of the huge crowd was a large tent and out of it suddenly stepped Guru Gobind Rai.

'I want a brave Sikh!' he shouted. He was waving a sword in the air. 'I want a brave Sikh who is willing to die for being a Sikh.'

The people were very worried. Had Guru Gobind Rai, their great leader, gone mad? 'I want a brave Sikh to step forward,' he shouted again. 'I want someone who is willing to die for being a Sikh.'

The crowd went very still. Then, quietly, one brave man stepped forward. 'I am willing to die for being a Sikh,' he said.

Guru Gobind Rai led the brave man into the tent. The crowd heard a swish and a thud and out of the tent came Guru Gobind Rai, still waving his sword, but this time it was dripping with blood! The crowd gasped.

'I want a brave Sikh!' shouted Guru Gobind Rai again, and again a brave man was led to the tent. Swish, thud! Five times this happened. Five brave men went into that tent.

Then the crowd was really surprised. After the fifth man had entered the tent, Guru Gobind Rai came out again, and he was followed by the five brave men. They were all perfectly well. And now they all wore special yellow clothes and proudly carried their own special swords. In the tent the crowd could see five dead goats.

Guru Gobind Rai had chosen his five bravest Sikhs to be the first five members of the special Sikh group called the Khalsa. From that day on they all took the name Singh which means 'lion'. So did Guru Gobind Rai, who became known as Guru Gobind Singh.

- Discuss the story (see prompts for discussion on page 128).
- Reinforce each story using the activities suggested on page 128.
- The children can retell the story to a partner or a group, or complete the drawing/ writing frame (see Figure 6.18 and the CD).

Figure 6.18

### Step 5 Evaluate

### Is it important for Sikhs to use *storytelling*?

**Questions to prompt discussion**

- Do you think that *storytelling* is a good way for Sikhs to teach people?
- What other way could be used?
- If they handed out papers or books for people to read would that be so good? Why? Why not?
- Would Sikhs learn as much?
- Would they understand so well?
- What difference does *storytelling* make to Sikhs?

 • Use the whiteboard or print on A4 sheets of paper the following statements for discussion (see Figure 6.20 and CD). Ask the children what they might say in each column. Provide the prompts below (Figure 6.19) for the children to consider and place on the charts.

everyone remembers the stories

people might be bored

people know how to behave

people think about important things in life

people can think about what God may be like

people would not learn so much

people might forget about important things in life

*Figure 6.19*

Sikhs use storytelling so that …

If Sikhs did not use storytelling …

*Figure 6.20*

## Resources on the CD

### Figures

6.1  Cards – When do you like to be told stories?
6.2  Cards – Which words go with the word "storytelling"?
6.3  Statements – *Was Jesus a good storyteller?*
6.4  Chart – *Was Jesus a good storyteller?*
6.5  Writing frame – *Here is a story Jesus told*
6.6  Writing frame – *The Buddha told stories because*
6.7  Statements – *Why did the Buddha tell stories?*
6.8  Chart – *Why did the Buddha tell stories?*
6.9  Writing frame – *Hindus tell stories because*
6.10  Statements –*Why do Hindus tell stories?*
6.11  Chart – *Why do Hindus tell stories?*
6.12  Writing frame – *Jewish people tell stories because*
6.13  Statements – *Why do Jews tell stories?*
6.14  Chart – *Why do Jews tell stories?*
6.15  Writing frame – *Muslim people tell stories because*
6.16  Statements – *Why do Muslims use storytelling?*
6.17  Chart – *Why do Muslims use storytelling?*
6.18  Writing frame – *Sikhs tell stories because*
6.19  Statements – *Why do Sikhs use storytelling?*
6.20  Chart – *Why do Sikhs use storytelling?*

### Artwork

A.  Joe, a Christian boy
B.  Elsa, a Buddhist girl
C.  Joshua, a Jewish boy
D.  Sita, a Hindu girl
E.  Fatima, a Muslim girl
F.  Amjid, a Sikh boy
31.  Jesus telling stories to a crowd
32.  The Buddha telling stories
33.  A Hindu telling stories
34.  A Sikh telling stories
35.  A Jewish father telling stories
36.  A Muslim telling stories

### Stories: Christian

*The Good Samaritan*
*The clever man and the silly man*
*The man who lost his sheep*

### Stories: Buddhist

*The blind men and the elephant*
*The five travellers*

### Stories: Hindu

*Lord Krishna protects all the people*
*Krishna and the buttermilk*

### Stories: Jewish

*The story of Esther*
*David and Goliath*

### Stories: Muslim

*Muhammad (pbuh) at the stream*
*Muhammad (pbuh) has rubbish thrown at him*

### Stories: Sikh

*Guru Nanak and the bowl of milk*
*Guru Gobind Rai and the five brave men*